What Does God Want From Me?

Mark Matlock

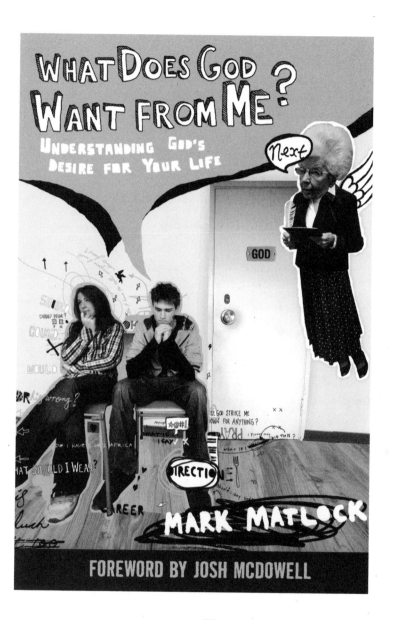

WHAT DOES GOD WANT FROM ME?

UNDERSTANDING GOD'S DESIRE FOR YOUR LIFE

MARK MATLOCK

FOREWORD BY JOSH MCDOWELL

ZONDERVAN®

www.invertbooks.com

What Does God Want From Me?: Understanding God's Desire for Your Life
Copyright © 2007 by Mark Matlock

Youth Specialties products, 300 S. Pierce St., El Cajon, CA 92020 are published by
Zondervan, 5300 Patterson Ave. SE, Grand Rapids, MI 49530.

Library of Congress Cataloging-in-Publication Data

Matlock, Mark.
   What does God want from me? : understanding God's desire for
your life / by Mark Matlock.
      p. cm.
   ISBN-10: 0-310-25815-4 (pbk.)
   ISBN-13: 978-0-310-25815-5 (pbk.)
   1. Teenagers--Religious life.   I. Title.
BV4531.3.M395 2007
248.8'3--dc22

                                                                    2006025329

This edition printed on acid-free paper.

All Scripture quotations, unless otherwise indicated, are taken from the *Holy Bible: New
International Version*. NIV. Copyright © 1973, 1978, 1984 by International Bible Society.
Used by permission of Zondervan. All rights reserved.

*Web site addresses listed in this book were current at the time of publication. Please con-
tact Youth Specialties via e-mail (YS@YouthSpecialties.com) to report URLs that are no
longer operational and provide replacement URLs if available.*

*Creative Team: Randy Southern, Holly Sharp/SharpSeven Design, Laura Gross, Heather
Haggerty, Ryan Sharp/SharpSeven Design*
Cover Design by Burnkit

Printed in the United States of America

06 07 08 09 10 11 12 • 22 21 20 19 18 17 16 15 14 13 12 11 10 9 8 7 6 5 4 3 2 1

Foreword   7

Chapter 1   What Do You Give the God Who Has   9
Everything?

Chapter 2   If You Really Love God, You'll Live Like   23
This...and Other Myths

Chapter 3   If You Love Me, You'll Obey Me   39

Chapter 4   And the Award for Greatest Commandment   51
Goes To...

Chapter 5   You Didn't Ask for Number Two, but I'll   77
Give It to You Anyway

Chapter 6   What Does It Look Like to "Do Justice"?   87

Chapter 7   You Just Gotta Love Mercy   103

Chapter 8   Walking Humbly with God   113

Chapter 9   People Versus Peoples: God's Commission   125
to Those Who Follow Him

Foreword

"What does God want from me?" is one of the most important questions a young person can ask. If we are clear on what God wants from us then we can make right choices with confidence. Lack of clarity, on the other hand, brings confusion, apprehension and consequences. This is why Paul said in 1 Corinthians 14:8, "If the trumpet does not sound a clear call, who will get ready for battle?"

In today's culture you are faced with a barrage of confusing voices from the media, your friends, your school, and many other places. While some of these voices may be encouraging you to seek what God wants, chances are, most are guiding you elsewhere. They are encouraging you to live for the moment, for pleasure, and for yourself. But God has a much bigger and better purpose for you—a purpose that will bring true meaning to your life, regardless of the circumstances you find yourself in.

Enter Mark Matlock and the book you now hold in your hand, *What Does God Want from Me?* Mark has done a masterful job of capturing the essence of what God wants from each of us, as well as providing steps for putting that truth into action.

If you want to focus your life on the best things God has for you, rather than merely settling for what seems to be good at the moment, then I could not recommend Mark's book more highly. My prayer is that you will read this book carefully and then pass it on to a friend. If more of us truly understood what God wanted from us, the world would be a better place.

Josh McDowell
Author/Speaker

CHAPTER 1

WHAT DO YOU GIVE THE GOD WHO HAS EVERYTHING?

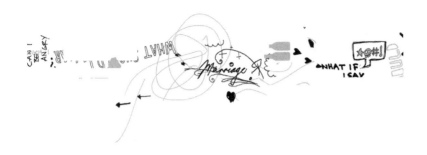

I was almost five years old when I first understood who Jesus was and what he'd done by dying on the cross for my sin. The details of where my awareness began and how it led to my decision to trust Christ as my Savior are a little murky, lost in the haze of time. But what I do know is that at the age of four and three quarters, I trotted down the aisle of my church to make public something I'd realized and discussed with my father the night before.

Mrs. McGannon, a nice older lady in my church, met me at the front of the sanctuary and escorted me to a room backstage. That's when I knew I was "in." I had a backstage pass to where the pastor and special music people hung out. Mrs. McGannon peppered me with questions and Scripture passages to make sure I "checked out" as the real deal. As I answered each question to her satisfaction, I could feel her excitement grow. I knew I was passing my test with flying colors.

WHAT DOES GOD WANT FROM ME?

Mrs. McGannon told me Jesus had been knocking on the door of my heart, and now I'd answered by opening the door and letting him in. She touched my chest and told me Jesus was going to live inside me. She asked me to repeat after her a prayer—a magic spell of sorts, I supposed—that would seal the deal in her eyes and, more importantly, in the eyes of God.

When we were done praying she gave me a certificate and a booklet I couldn't read—except for the title, which had "John" in it. That was exciting to me because John was the name of one of my friends. I walked out of the backstage area and experienced something I could not have imagined. People were genuinely excited about the little walk I'd taken to the front of the church. Some hugged me; others cheered. My grandma Nora had tears in her eyes.

None of my friends were present. They were all on the playground. Meanwhile their parents were hugging me and telling me that someday their kids would have to take the walk too. Sure enough, over the next several months many of my friends did exactly that. I couldn't say what the walk meant to them or whether they felt pressured to do it because of my short pioneering trip, but there's one thing I did know: No matter what the people at church thought, my little walk wasn't nearly as important to me as the realization that prompted it, that I wanted to follow Jesus. I took my newfound desire pretty seriously—at least as seriously as my almost-five-year-old mind could handle.

When I got home from church that night, I asked my mom why my heart was still beating. Puzzled, she asked

What Do You Give the God Who Has Everything?

what I meant. I said, "If I opened the door of my heart to Jesus, why is he still knocking?" Obviously I had much to learn on my spiritual journey.

Years later, during my sophomore year of high school, I began to sense there was something more I should be doing with my life. People in my church and various Christian speakers made me feel as though I was obligated to do something for God. They made me feel guilty for taking God's free gift of salvation and not giving anything back.

Their expectations reminded me of the time Jerry, a friend at school, gave me a box of Jujubes. I thought, *How cool, this guy could be a great friend.* Later, however, Jerry used his gift of candy against me when I wouldn't let him copy off my homework. Jerry's gift had strings attached. Strictly speaking, it was free. But it also bound me (in his eyes) to do things I didn't want to do.

I began to wonder if that's how Jesus worked too. Was he a slick salesman, offering a gift that seemed almost too good to be true and then obligating people with the fine print at the bottom of a contract?

Follow Me

The Gospels make it clear that Jesus was totally upfront about what it takes to follow him. He left no doubt as to the degree of commitment he required. He instructed his 12 disciples to leave what they were doing and join him—not for a day or a week or even a month, but forever. Peter,

James, John, and Andrew understood the seriousness of their decisions when they dropped their fishing nets—and their fathers—to follow Jesus. They left their source of income lying on the ground (Matthew 4:18-22).

Later, when a rich young man expressed interest in following Jesus, Jesus told him to sell everything he had first (Luke 18:18-25). The young man walked away sad because he couldn't make the sacrifice. If you read the passage, you'll notice that Jesus didn't go after him. He let the young man leave. It seems Jesus didn't want someone following him who wasn't prepared to sacrifice everything and endure anything.

As extreme as it sounds, that stipulation wasn't a problem for me as a teenager. In my youthful zeal, I wasn't bothered by the cost or pain of following Jesus. While it seemed certain people wanted to make me feel obligated to do something for Christ, I didn't feel it was a duty. It was something I *wanted* to do.

Think about the last Father's Day gift you gave, if you can remember it. Chances are, you didn't put a lot of thought into it. For many people, Father's Day is more of an obligation than a celebration. They don't buy gifts for their dads because they *want* to; they do it because they've been told they *have* to. Now that I'm a father, I have to admit that attitude bothers me a little more than it used to.

For some of us, the problem is that we don't know what our fathers really want. They seem to have almost everything they need, and what they don't have is often beyond

What Do You Give the God Who Has Everything?

our ability to give. One year I solved that problem when I discovered my dad wanted a particular Bible study software package. The problem was, his computer wasn't powerful enough to run it. That gave me an idea: my brothers and I would pool our resources and buy him the computer he needed.

Obviously this was no small gift. I was just starting out in ministry and my brothers were in college. Saving the necessary amount of money took several months, but we did it. We bought the computer and we couldn't wait to give it to him. While previous Father's Day gifts had been given out of obligation, this one was different. We were excited to give it. We'd carefully chosen the present and made personal sacrifices to purchase it. It was the most difficult gift I'd ever given and the one that cost me the most; yet it was the one I took the most joy in giving.

Could the same thing be said of our devotion and service to God? There are times when we feel obligated to give something back to him. And we do so without much feeling or personal investment. Other times, however—when we get a sense of what he truly desires—we realize that no sacrifice on our part is too great when it comes to fulfilling those desires.

The question is, what are those desires? What does God want? What does he need?

What Does God Need?

If that question seems absurd to you, you're not alone. Check out the Lord's words in Psalm 50:9-15:

> I have no need of a bull from your stall or of goats from your pens, for every animal of the forest is mine, and the cattle on a thousand hills. I know every bird in the mountains, and the creatures of the field are mine. If I were hungry I would not tell you, for the world is mine, and all that is in it. Do I eat the flesh of bulls or drink the blood of goats? Sacrifice thank offerings to God, fulfill your vows to the Most High, and call upon me in the day of trouble; I will deliver you, and you will honor me.

In this psalm Asaph describes a courtroom drama in which God has called the people of the earth to account for their lives. One of his accusations is that people have misunderstood what he wants from them. God had put a sacrificial system in place to remind the people of Israel of their sin—and the fact that blood was required to forgive it (Hebrews 9:22). He wanted them to be sorrowful about their sin and thankful for his forgiveness.

There was nothing magical about the animal blood itself; it was just a reminder that God would provide the blood needed to save the people. The people, however, mistakenly believed that what God wanted was the actual animals and food they offered. They overlooked the attitude of the heart God wanted from them.

What Do You Give the God Who Has Everything?

God responded by making it clear that he was not in need and that even if he ever was in need, the human race would be the last place he would turn for help. Think about it. When you need money, you go to someone who has it, right? I typically started with my parents. If that failed, a call to my grandparents usually solved the problem. God won't turn to us because we have nothing to offer him. We can't give him anything that's not already his. He doesn't even need our worship. He's God. He needs nothing.

That sacrificial system he set up for Israel has now been rendered unnecessary because Christ shed his blood for us—once and for all. However, God is still concerned about the attitudes of our hearts. He wants us to be genuinely thankful for all he's done for us. It shouldn't be hard for us to do.

The Art of Appreciation

Have you ever admired someone? When I was eight, I saw *Star Wars: Episode IV—A New Hope* for the first time. The film changed the way my friends and I played. Instead of guns and bows and arrows, we imagined blasters and light sabers. At recess we competed to see who could make the best Darth Vader sound. The winner got to play the villain.

I became interested in the man who made the movie, George Lucas. I wanted to be like him. He created whole new worlds to dream about and creatures I never could have imagined. I read magazine articles and a book about his life. I decided I wanted to be a filmmaker; and I started my own movie company called Animated World, which was dedicated to producing the most fantastic special effects films known to man. Of course, if I'd ever run into George Lucas on the street, I would have been speechless—too afraid to even tell him how much I appreciate his work.

While George Lucas gave me some ideas to dream about, God has done so much more. He made the world I live in (Genesis 1:1). He created humankind (Genesis 2:7). What's more, even though I've offended his perfection and holiness with my sin (Romans 3:23), he made it possible to escape the punishment of death because he gave his son to die for me (Romans 6:23). God has changed my life more than George Lucas ever could. On top of everything else, God calls me his friend (John 15:13-15). I don't have to be intimidated by him. I can approach him as I would someone I know very well, even though his power is awesome.

Such loving acts call for serious appreciation. If you're interested in showing God the appreciation he deserves, you need to ask yourself two questions: *What do I know about God?* and *What do I think about what he's done for me?* If you ponder those questions long enough, you'll develop a desire to do something in response. My admiration of George Lucas caused me to read books about him and pursue the things he was interested in. I know people who admire certain musicians. They show their admiration by dressing like the artists and trying to learn all they can about them. They spend their money to buy CDs and support the artists' favorite causes. I know students who admire certain athletes. They show their admiration by watching the players' games, wearing their jerseys, and buying whatever shoes they endorse. The

What Do You Give the God Who Has Everything?

bottom line is, when you *really* admire someone, it changes the way you think and the way you live certain areas of your life. It can influence the decisions you make and the way you spend your money.

The same applies to our appreciation for God. The question is: In what ways should our thoughts, actions, and decision-making be changed? Or, to put it another way: What does God want from his admirers?

What Does God Want?

Early in the Bible we get a clue as to God's preferences. The clue can be found in Genesis 4:2-8, the story of Cain and Abel. Both brothers gave gifts to God, but each one received a different response from him. See for yourself:

> Later she gave birth to his brother Abel. Now Abel kept flocks, and Cain worked the soil. In the course of time Cain brought some of the fruits of the soil as an offering to the Lord. But Abel brought fat portions from some of the firstborn of his flock. The Lord looked with favor on Abel and his offering, but on Cain and his offering he did not look with favor. So Cain was very angry, and his face was downcast. Then the Lord said to Cain, "Why are you angry? Why is your face downcast? If you do what is right, will you not be accepted? But if you do not do what is right, sin is crouching at your door; it desires to have you, but you must master it." Now Cain said to his brother Abel, "Let's go out to the field." And while they

were in the field, Cain attacked his brother Abel and killed him.

It's an intense story—and a confusing one too. After all, what was wrong with Cain's gift? A couple passages in the New Testament shed some light on the issue:

> By faith Abel offered God a better sacrifice than Cain did. By faith he was commended as a righteous man, when God spoke well of his offerings. And by faith he still speaks, even though he is dead…And without faith it is impossible to please God, because anyone who comes to him must believe that he exists and that he rewards those who earnestly seek him. (Hebrews 11:4, 6)

Abel's gift pleased God because of the faith that accompanied it—something that Cain's gift apparently lacked. Perhaps Abel was active in his desire to know God and to please him with his life, whereas Cain had no real interest in knowing who God was or in delighting him. Cain was simply doing the duty of giving God a gift; but Abel delighted in serving God because Abel understood who God was.

Then 1 John 3:12 tells us that not only was Abel right in his living, but Cain was in fact evil. His gift was offered only because he felt he should:

> Do not be like Cain, who belonged to the evil one and murdered his brother. And why did he murder him? Because his own actions were evil and his brother's were righteous.

What Do You Give the God Who Has Everything?

I have to confess that many times I've given God gifts that were more like Cain's than Abel's. I've gone to church because my parents made me feel guilty about not going. I've given money for God's work because I felt I had to or because I was afraid God would take something away from me if I didn't. I've done service projects in the Lord's name only because a girl I was interested in was going on the trip too.

My freshman year in high school, Wendy Colman gave a testimony about the importance of going on a certain service project. That same day I signed up for the project because Wendy was a babe. I remember how every time I saw her at church I'd say, "Hey, Wendy, sure can't wait for the service project!" I didn't notice it at the time, but Wendy never really said much to me about it. Finally the big day for the trip arrived. As we loaded the vans, I kept asking, "Has anyone seen Wendy? I'd sure hate for us to leave her behind." Finally, one of the leaders said, "Oh...no...Wendy's not coming on this trip."

My reply went something like this: "Well, if Wendy's not coming on this stupid trip, then what the heck am I doing here?" Everyone looked at me like I was an idiot. The truth is, I was an idiot. I was going on the trip for the wrong reason; and as it tends to go with those kinds of things, I got out of it just exactly what I put into it.

I guess what you have to determine at this point is whether or not you really care about what God has done for you. If you do, and I assume you're somewhat interested or you wouldn't be reading this book, then you need to ask yourself what you can do for God that would show your thankfulness. While God is more interested in the motive behind a gift than the gift itself, my guess is that the gift matters too.

When I was a kid, a friend and I were at a 7-Eleven store with his mom. I wanted candy, but his mother wouldn't let us buy any. When we got home, my friend pulled a piece of candy from his pocket and said, "Here, I got this for you." When I asked how he did it, he told me he'd put it in his pocket when nobody was looking. His act was selfless (he didn't cop any candy for himself), but that didn't change the fact that I didn't want him to steal for me.

In the next few chapters, we'll discover what God wants—and doesn't want—from us.

Questions to Ponder

1. In this chapter Mark recounted the events leading up to the moment when he realized who Jesus was and what he had done. Can you remember when you came to realize you could put your trust in Christ's death on the cross as payment for your sin?

2. Mark's parents, his church youth group, and a woman named Mrs. McGannon helped shape his understanding of who Jesus is and what he meant to Mark's life. Who has helped shape your understanding of Jesus?

What Do You Give the God Who Has Everything?

3. Have you ever felt pressure to "do" something for God? If so, what? Why did you feel pressure?

4. Like Cain, have you ever given something to or done something for God with a wrong heart? If so, do you feel as though you have peace with God about that now?

5. Mark talked about his appreciation and admiration for George Lucas. Whom do you really admire? Mark read books about George Lucas, and he even made extremely low-budget movies in order to be like him. How does your admiration for a certain person affect your life?

6. Can you honestly say you have an admiration or adoration for God? If so, how has it made a difference in your life?

CHAPTER 2

IF YOU REALLY LOVE GOD, YOU'LL LIVE LIKE THIS... AND OTHER MYTHS

Much of my life growing up was spent attending church or church-related activities. I joined choirs, sang solos in church, and eventually became a leader in my youth group. For the most part, I was a good boy—a good *Christian* boy. And like most good Christian boys, I was known not so much for what I did but for what I *didn't* do.

Since my short walk down the church aisle, I'd learned that good boys didn't cuss, drink alcohol, smoke cigarettes, do drugs, or have sex outside of marriage. They also were careful about what music they listened to (Christian only) and never watched movies that were inappropriate (especially R-rated movies). My list of don'ts wasn't very long, so I found it easy to stay away from off-limit activities—even the ones my friends really struggled with.

That didn't mean I was always happy about the things I felt I couldn't do. When I was in elementary school, one of my relatives gave me some records—specifically, some non-

Christian rock albums. And I liked them. I enjoyed rocking out to the music in my bedroom on my plastic guitar and Muppet drum set.

One morning while I was waiting outside for my ride to school, I saw my albums in the garbage can. *Holy cow!* I thought. *A serious mistake has been made. Somehow my records were accidentally placed in the trash!* Curiously, my Bible story records and Sesame Street albums weren't in there—just those other ones from my relative.

I could see the carpool station wagon coming down the street. I had only moments to act. I grabbed the stack of records (which was huge and heavy) and staggered back to the house. "Mom!" I blurted. "These records fell in the trash can. But it's okay, I saved them."

My mom and dad looked at each other. "Mark, we threw those away on purpose," Dad said. Tears filled my eyes. How could this be? My father stood up, took the records from me, and walked me out to the street where the honking station wagon was waiting. "We'll get you some new records," he promised. "We just don't like these."

"But I like jumping on my bed and screaming out loud while I'm listening to them," I replied.

"You'll like the new records too," he assured me. "Now get in the car and go to school."

If You Really Love God, You'll Live Like This...and Other Myths

As the car drove away, I plastered my face to the window and watched as my dad returned the records to the garbage can.

To this day I can't remember what records were tossed or what bands played on them. But I do remember that the new records my parents purchased at the Christian bookstore weren't quite the same. In time, I grew to like the new records, but musically I was out of touch. None of my friends at school knew who Bill Gaither or Dallas Holmes was. But I was cool with it. I wanted to be a good Christian boy.

The World

Like it or not, some people have very strong feelings about how Christians should and shouldn't live...and act...and dress. There's nothing wrong with strong opinions—except when there's little or no evidence in Scripture or in the life of Christ to support them.

I'll never forget how one Sunday morning I watched an older woman in our church verbally attack my friend Robert for wearing an earring and a Mohawk. "You look like the world, young man," she said, pointing a wrinkled, bony finger at him.

I thought about her words. What exactly was "the world"? Most of the people in the world I lived in didn't wear their hair like Robert did. And few men in my world wore earrings. So if the world she spoke of was something defined by the majority, then Robert wasn't part of it. The other people in my church were the ones dressing like the world because they were wearing the latest fashions. White-collar criminals and evil world leaders I'd seen on television favored the coat-and-tie look sported by my pastor. Did that qualify as a "worldly" look? The idea fascinated me. What was this "world" she was talking about?

In John 17:15-18, Jesus offers a prayer for his disciples in which he refers to the world. Here's what he says:

> My prayer is not that you take them out of the world but that you protect them from the evil one. They are not of the world, even as I am not of it. Sanctify them by the truth; your word is truth. As you sent me into the world, I have sent them into the world.

It's clear Jesus didn't consider his disciples to be part of this world, even though they were living in it. So what world is Jesus talking about? I don't think he meant the planet. Other passages, such as Colossians 2:8, 20 and 1 John 2:15-17, imply that the "world" is the system of beliefs and behaviors that people have adopted. Not necessarily the people them-selves, but the way they think and live.

That definition of "world" makes sense when we read the familiar words of Romans 12:2:

> Do not conform any longer to the pattern of this world, but be transformed by the renewing of your mind. Then you will be able to test and approve what God's will is—his good, pleasing and perfect will.

If You Really Love God, You'll Live Like This...and Other Myths

If the world is a set of ideas and behaviors, then it's God's desire that we not allow those ideas and behaviors to shape or form us.

And if that's what that elderly woman from my church had in mind years ago, she was way off base. She assumed people wearing Mohawks and earrings were rebellious toward God; thus, if Robert dressed in that manner, he was being like the world. The truth is, the way he dressed had little to do with the way he thought or behaved. Yes, some people dress differently to rebel against the establishment and the status quo, but the status quo is what Jesus would deem as the "world." God wants us to live extraordinary lives—according to his truth.

In almost every church, you'll find people like the one who accosted my friend. They aren't bad people; they just tend to focus on the wrong things from time to time.

A New Way of Life

Acts 15 records a monumental shift in thinking, as far as God's people were concerned. If we look to the Old Testament, we see that God predominantly made himself known to the world through the people of Israel. After the death and resurrection of Jesus, things changed in a big way. The Holy Spirit descended and began living inside of people—and not just Jewish people. Christ's sacrifice was for everyone, whether they were Jewish or not. (By the way, non-Jewish people are called "Gentiles" in the Bible.)

In the Old Testament, God gave the people of Israel a set of laws about how to govern themselves. The official name for that arrangement is a *theocracy*, which means that just about every instruction regarding how they should live came directly from God. Jesus, however, showed a new way of living that wasn't bound by the cultural limitations the Jews had lived by. Jesus wasn't taking anything away from Jewish law; instead, he fulfilled it with his life. You might say Jesus came to show the next phase of his relationship with the people he created.

The shift created an interesting—and controversial—multiethnic dynamic in the church. On the one hand, you had Jews who'd been worshipping God their entire lives and living according to the cultural laws he'd given to them. On the other hand, you had Gentiles who were new to the worship of God. Both groups were following Christ, but they had different ideas about how things should be done.

Some Jewish Christians believed that all followers of Christ needed to be circumcised. (If you don't know what circumcision is—look it up. I'm not telling you about it here.) You can imagine how the new Christian men who were uncircumcised felt about that rule.

Paul and Barnabas traveled to Jerusalem to talk with the apostles and church elders about the issue. When they got there, they gave a report about all the things God was doing through them and in the lives of the Gentiles. Some new Christians who had once been part of the Pharisees argued that the Gentiles had to be circumcised in order to obey the Law of Moses (the first five books of the Old Testament).

After carefully considering the matter, the apostles and elders decided not to complicate Christianity for the Gentiles by making them follow all the laws given to Moses. Instead, they narrowed the list down to four requirements. The Gentiles should avoid—

1. Food sacrificed to idols,

2. Eating blood,

3. The meat of strangled animals, and

4. Sexual immorality.

(*Note to my mom and dad: please note they said nothing about non-Christian music.*)

There you have it. The entire Law of Moses boiled down to just four instructions. The leaders of the church didn't want to burden the Gentiles with anything beyond that.

One of Us

At the heart of the controversy was the issue of identification. Jewish men were identifiable because of circumcision. They, in turn, wanted to be able to identify others as belonging to the one true living God. That desire to be able to identify other believers is still strong today.

People constantly size each other up—especially where the Christian faith is concerned. They create their own personal guidelines and checklists for determining whether someone is acting like a Christian or not. For example, some Christians believe it's wrong to have a tattoo or watch R-rated movies. And while there may be some good reasons to avoid such things, the truth is, those actions have little to do with whether or not a person belongs to Christ and is following him. Remember, many Christians will tell you what they think God wants you to do, but it doesn't mean that's what he's really looking for.

During my junior high years, I realized some of my friends weren't nearly as serious about being a good boy as I was. That realization led me to wonder if maybe I was...well, *better* than they were. It didn't take long for me to reach a conclusion. While my friends' actions were enticing (I mean, who wouldn't want to make out with a hot girl on the dark church bus during a return trip from a day at the beach?), I was comfortable with abstaining as long as I kept my moral superiority over them.

My Christianity was wrapped up in the things I didn't do. Almost imperceptibly I drifted from genuinely loving Christ as a kindergartner to being a real pain.

I was brimming with arrogance, conceit, pride, conde-scension, and selfishness. I believed I was right in every cir-cumstance, no matter what anyone else said. What's worse, I was often rewarded for my attitude. I won Bible trivia con-tests and always had a ready answer for any question—so much so that many teachers asked me not to answer so quickly, in order to give the other kids time to respond. I considered it a real compliment when a group leader would say, "Does someone—other than Mark—want to answer?" or "Mark, I see your hand, but I want to give someone else a shot." I really didn't care if the other people talked or not, since I figured I was always right. Plus, being the "Bible nerd" in church made me a real "babe magnet"!

What I didn't understand was that while God had definitely given commands for his people to follow, there were other things in Scripture that weren't so clear to all people. What's more, many people had opinions that had little or nothing to do with God and what he'd revealed.

Some people "major in the minors." That is, they get passionate about things that simply don't matter. For some people, sports are a passion. I know people (and you know them too) whose moods are directly connected to the score of their favorite team's last game—or to their fantasy sports statistics. They become depressed or elated based on how their teams performed.

Overseas, soccer fans become crazed and incite riots over games. When a friend of mine visited Turkey, he was often asked, "Which team do you support?" To many people, team loyalty is what measures a person—what gives him his identity.

What gives a Christian her identity? Or, to put it another way: What matters to God where we're concerned? In order to answer that question, we need to identify three elements of Scripture: commands, applications, and opinions.

COMMANDS: THE ESSENTIALS

Commands are the truths we stand on, the ones that distinguish Christianity from other faiths. Those truths include the fact that faith in Jesus saves us from our sins...that Christ was God in human form...that he rose from the dead to prove our faith in him isn't futile (1 Corinthians 15). The doctrines of the trinity, the authority of Scripture, the image of God in humans, the human race's need for a savior, and the Great Commission form the foundation of our values, our choices, and our lives.

The word *command* is often viewed negatively in our culture. That's too bad because Jesus used the word quite often. He told us that if we love him, we will obey his commands. He also told us in the Great Commission that we should make disciples of all nations, baptizing them and teaching them all that he commanded.

When it comes to commands, two stand out—the two Jesus believed were most important: love the Lord your God with everything you are, and love your neighbor as yourself.

APPLICATIONS: A CULTURAL THING

Applications are beliefs we derive from Scripture that are shaped by our culture and community. While I believe there is only one correct interpretation of Scripture—that is, God meant what he said and was clear about it—I also realize there are many ways we can apply that truth to our lives. And these ways may differ from culture to culture and from person to person.

Understanding culture and community is essential to living wisely. I grew up in California and spent quite a bit of time at the beach. Because of the beach culture, I saw members of the opposite sex wearing swimsuits, often showing a lot of flesh. The standards of modesty in my culture were very different from standards in other parts of the country. So when I started working in youth ministry around the nation, I found it very odd that several camps didn't allow guys and girls to swim together. They called it "mixed bathing" (which makes swimming sound really creepy). I must admit I used to think those camp organizers were seriously backward until I realized that many of them came from small, agricultural communities where the standards of modesty were different from what I was used to.

Cultural applications are not simply neutral—they have real impact! When I visited India, many Christian young men wanted to hold my hand as we walked down the street. In their culture, that was totally appropriate. But the feelings I had about it were most uncomfortable!

On a trip to another country, some girls in my group couldn't understand why the missionaries asked them to refrain from wearing makeup. Not understanding the cultural interpretations of modesty, they ignored the missionaries' instruction. Later, they were shocked to find men groping them and copping feels as they passed by. They discovered that in that particular culture, only prostitutes wore makeup. So those men were simply sampling the merchandise!

In the United States, many Christian communities frown on drinking alcohol—period. While the Bible gives a strong command against drunkenness, there are other interpretations as to whether it's justifiable for Christians to drink. When my brother Jeremy traveled to Ireland to speak at a church, he was surprised when the pastor took him to a pub to have a pint with the deacons and other church members the night before. Different communities and cultures have different interpretations of what is appropriate, based on their understanding of the Bible.

OPINIONS: IT'S PERSONAL

Opinions are personal preferences that don't carry the weight of commands or applications. It doesn't matter whether you like pepperoni or Italian sausage, thin crust or hand-tossed, or how many levels of angels you believe exist in heaven. Some things are simply not worth getting into an argument over.

Because of my personal opinions about Scripture and about how I should pursue holiness in my life, I may choose to live differently than other Christians do. I may choose not to drink alcohol when I'm around a friend who struggles with it. My wife may choose to wear different swimsuits depending on which culture she's living in.

If, however, I tell someone else he must make the same choice I make, then I become legalistic. Many of our opinions aren't worthy of being imposed or even discussed with others. They may help *me* live for Christ more effectively, but another person may not experience the same results.

You'll find that some people are too passionate about their opinions. When a friend of mine came back from a spring break trip with a tattoo of a cross on his arm, another friend just couldn't believe he would do such a thing. He was appalled by the tattoo, and the topic always seemed to come up in conversations between the two of them. Eventually it fractured their relationship.

On the other hand, some people aren't passionate enough about the essentials. I know people who don't have a clue what they believe. They don't have a firm foundation of truth to stand on, so they don't have essential convictions (commands) to live by and share with others. They just have opinions, and they aren't too sure about those either.

With that understanding, it makes sense that God wants us to obey his commands, make careful applications, and be wise about our opinions. The next several chapters will explore the commands God has given us and help us understand the freedom and joy that come from following them.

Questions to Ponder

1. What are some things that might cause you to suspect someone is a Christian?

2. Have you ever been surprised by something you saw a Christian do? If so, what was it? How did it make you feel?

3. What are some things people say Christians *shouldn't* do? Are they right or wrong to believe this way? Can you find any evidence (or lack of evidence) in the Bible to support your opinion?

4. Do you ever feel as though you miss out on things because you're a Christian? If so, can you share some examples? Does not being able to do those things bother you?

5. What do you think of Mark's breakdown of commands, applications, and opinions? Do you see any problems with that kind of thinking? Do you see any benefits? How could such an understanding help Christians work better together?

CHAPTER 3

IF YOU LOVE ME, YOU'LL OBEY ME

During my senior year of high school, I was invited to Sacramento for a leadership forum with other students from all over California. I was selected to represent the students of the Los Angeles area. All alone, I got on a plane and flew north. At the hotel where the forum was held, it quickly became apparent that everyone present—all 80 invitees—knew each other...with one exception. I didn't know anyone.

I moved around the room, looking for someone who might take me in as the outsider and introduce me to the others. I'd learned early on that it was important to hook up with the right people in a situation like that. Otherwise, you got stuck with losers the entire time. The problem was, the losers were the ones most likely to take you in.

Maybe you've seen it happen with new kids at school. When the teacher asks for someone to show the new student the ropes, some nice but generally unknown person with no social standing will volunteer. That person gives the new kid a tour, eats lunch with him, and introduces him around. If the two are a match socially, they might remain friends. But more often than not, it's only a matter of days before the new kid finds his own "kind." If the kid is rich or athletic, he'll hook up with others who are like him. If the kid was a trouble magnet at his previous school, he'll find the troublemakers to hang out with.

In Sacramento I wasn't just looking for people to talk to. I was looking for the "right" people to talk to. As it turned out, there weren't any losers in the room—except me. Those people were the cream of the crop—the best of the best at their schools. Fortunately for me, they were also very nice and took me in.

Having grown up in the same city and attended the same church (which my grandparents helped start) my whole life, it was strange being in a place where nobody knew anything about me. I could have made up anything about myself and no one would have known the truth. I could have told people my dad was one of the lesser-known astronauts. I could have passed myself off as being rich, poor, smart, dumb—whatever I wanted. But instead of trying to be something I wasn't, I found myself being more like the person I really wanted to be. You see, while my new acquaintances were all good and kind, it became apparent that few of them were followers of Christ. And as I talked and moved among them, I felt my Christlike nature start to come out. Gone was the teenage Pharisee I had become back home. In his place was a guy whose actions were starting to match his beliefs.

If You Love Me, You'll Obey Me

I'd brought my Bible with me and decided maybe I should read it for a change. So I opened to the gospel of Matthew and started reading about Jesus. That's when I realized that while I'd always considered myself a follower of Christ, my life didn't look much like that of the man who saved me. Jesus had a way of loving people (and upsetting them) that was quite different from the way I interacted with others. I realized how far my life had drifted from the example Christ set. I'd been spending so much energy "not" doing certain things that I'd neglected to *do* the things that were truly the marks of a disciple. I may have believed all the right things and made a stand for the right causes, but the way I went about it looked nothing like the Jesus I was reading about. In Sunday school I'd heard so many stories about Jesus that I'd never really looked at his life for myself. And when I finally did, I discovered that Jesus was less like a fairy tale, and more like something very real.

I moved on to the gospel of John and came across some words of Jesus in chapter 14 that really convicted me:

If you love me, you will obey what I command…If anyone loves me, he will obey my teaching. My Father will love him, and we will come to him and make our home with him. He who does not love me will not obey my teaching. These words you hear are not my own; they belong to the Father who sent me. (John 14:15, 23-24)

For the first time, I realized that while God most certainly wanted me to have the right beliefs, he also wanted me to be obedient. I'd been told many times that following Christ was about a relationship, not rules. But Jesus' words in John 14 make it clear that the evidence of a loving relationship with him is obedience in following his rules. Jesus says flat out, if you love me you'll obey my teachings and commands.

My son, Dax, is a great kid, but he's a little boy who's still learning about life. And like all little boys, he makes mistakes. One day he was being particularly difficult to be around. First, he wouldn't do his chores around the house. Then when we went shopping, he whined and complained about things I wouldn't buy him.

On the way home from the store, he told me he loved me. I said, "No, Dax, you don't."

He laughed and said, "Sure I do, Dad. I love you."

I replied, "Dax, if you loved me, you'd obey me."

Had my love changed for Dax during his spell of disobedience? Absolutely not. Would his obedience make me love him more? Absolutely not. What was in question was not my love for Dax, but his love for me. If he really cared for me and loved me, he would have shown it with his obedience. Likewise, in John 14 it's not Christ's love that's in question—it's ours. He loves us—absolutely. But if we want to show him that we love him, we'll obey him.

Show Your Love

My wife doesn't like chocolate very much. If I gave her chocolate as a gift, she wouldn't appreciate it—no matter how good the chocolate was or how much care I took in selecting it. My wife prefers thoughtful surprises. She likes it when I take the time to write her little love notes. So if I want to show her my love, I'll write her a note. In order to effectively express my feelings, I have to know what she appreciates. The same is true when it comes to God.

Too often we try to give God things he doesn't appreciate. We try to do things he never asked us to do. If obedience and love are connected, then we aren't showing him love when we do only what we *think* he wants. What we're really doing is giving him gifts on our terms.

Luke 10 describes a visit Jesus made to the home of Mary and Martha. Imagine having Jesus as a houseguest. Sure, it would have been an honor; but it also would have been quite a bit of work because Jesus always brought a crowd with him. There were the 12 disciples, the other followers who traveled with him, and the paparazzi types who hung out and waited to see him do something spectacular or say something profound.

To get an idea of what a home visit from Jesus was like, check out Luke 5:17-26. The crowds were so heavy around the house of Jesus' host that no one outside could get in to where Jesus was. Instead, people crowded around the windows and doors. Among the crowd was a group of men who wanted Jesus to heal a friend of theirs who couldn't walk. Unable to get close to Jesus, they improvised. They climbed on top of the house, tore a hole in the roof, and lowered their friend to Jesus.

The situation at Mary and Martha's house was probably just as chaotic. Martha, ever the good hostess, kept herself busy serving appetizers and drinks to her guests. Her sister Mary, however, did nothing to help. In fact, Mary spent the entire visit sitting at Jesus' feet, leaving Martha to do all the work. (Anyone who has a lazy brother or sister—or lab partner—can empathize.)

Martha got angry and went straight to Jesus with her complaint. "Lord, don't you care that my sister has left me to do the work by myself?" she asked. "Tell her to help me!"

Imagine Mary's embarrassment and nervousness over her sister's accusation. She had no idea how Jesus would react. Would he humiliate her? Would he send her to the kitchen?

Here's what he did: "Martha, Martha," the Lord answered, "you are worried and upset about many things, but only one thing is needed. Mary has chosen what is better, and it will not be taken away from her" (Luke 10:38-42).

Martha certainly wasn't expecting that response. Essentially, Jesus told her that while her preparations were appreciated, party planning wasn't really the most rewarding thing she could be doing with her time. I can picture Jesus saying, "Look, Martha, it's great to be in your home, but I'm only here for a short time. Be with me—that's what's important. I'm not hungry and I don't need anything to drink. Just be with me and learn from me while I'm here."

If You Love Me, You'll Obey Me

How often do we miss the best thing we could be doing because we're busy doing something that's just "good"? Martha had good intentions. She wasn't doing anything evil. She just wasn't doing what was best. Jesus wants our best—on his terms, not ours. Many people busy themselves doing good things at church and at home, but they miss the best. Jesus says, "If you love me, you'll obey me." Obedience is always the best.

What's Love Got to Do with It?

If obedience is good, then obedience done with a spirit of love is off the charts. For proof of that, you need look no further than the apostle Paul's first letter to the church of Corinth.

The Corinthian Christians often argued about which spiritual gifts were the best. It was strictly an ego thing. Everyone wanted to be more important to God than the next guy. In the process of promoting themselves and their gifts, the Corinthians lost their spirit of love. The apostle Paul wanted them to know that without love, it didn't matter how great a person's gift or talent was—it was useless to God. Look at Paul's words in 1 Corinthians 12:31–13:3:

> And now I will show you the most excellent way. If I speak in the tongues of men and of angels, but have not love, I am only a resounding gong or a clanging cymbal. If I have the gift of prophecy and can fathom all mysteries and all knowledge, and if I have a faith that can move

mountains, but have not love, I am nothing. If I give all I possess to the poor and surrender my body to the flames, but have not love, I gain nothing.

Imagine being able to speak any language—fluently and eloquently. How cool would that be? Paul emphasizes the fact that without love, no one can communicate properly. Ask a happily married couple about the secret of their successful relationship, and they'll probably say communication. But in 1 Corinthians 13, we see that the real secret to good communication is love.

I think about situations in which people get angry while trying to tell others about the love of Christ. (It happens occasionally at family gatherings, when a well-meaning believer tries to convert a non-Christian relative.) It doesn't matter how true your words are; if love is not the motivation, then they won't be heard.

Love Gives Our Communication Impact

Imagine being able to recall everything you've ever learned and being able to apply it in ways that solve the world's greatest problems and mysteries. Once again, it's a pretty cool prospect. However, Paul says knowledge and insight are worthless without love.

I've seen Christians get into incredible, intellectual arguments about why Christianity should be considered true. In fact, I've been in the middle of several such arguments. But

If You Love Me, You'll Obey Me

I've discovered that if love isn't present, it doesn't matter how persuasive my facts are. The truth is, not one person I've argued with has ever said, "You win the debate. I'll trust Christ." So I've learned to say, "Look, I don't want to argue. I'm happy to answer your questions, but this isn't about winning a debate. I want you to know that God loves you. I've experienced his love and I want you to experience it too."

LOVE MAKES OUR KNOWLEDGE USEFUL

I've always thought that moving mountains would be an awesome accomplishment. The Bible says if I have enough faith, I can. There are people who spend their entire lives doing things for God—but they're doing them out of a sense of obligation, not love. They do "churchy" things, volunteering for ministries that raise their personal profile or that conveniently fit into their schedule. They do good things, but not necessarily the things God wants them to do. They lack obedience. And without obedience, love is impossible. Without love, faith is trivial.

LOVE MAKES OUR FAITH SIGNIFICANT

I've always wanted to win the lottery so I could support worthy causes. But I don't think God needs lottery money to get his work done. While it would be great to have a lot to give, dollar amounts aren't important. Being obedient with what we have and joyfully giving God the portion he requires is all he wants from us. Some people dutifully put their money in the offering plate every Sunday without a second thought. For them, God's work is just another financial obligation. Their attitude is anything but joyful and loving. As a result, their giving is worthless in God's eyes.

Love Makes Our Gifts Valuable

As I wrap up this chapter, let me offer one more example from my own life. When I was a kid, my brothers and I took an unusual approach to Mother's Day gift buying. Usually, our presents to Mom had a kitchen theme, perhaps because we viewed her as our meal ticket. One year it was a donut maker. Another year it was a snow cone machine. Whatever sounded good to us—that's what she got. One year we broke away from our kitchen tradition and bought her a video game—so she could enjoy peace and quiet while we were busy playing it.

Mom always smiled and thanked us for the gifts, but she knew how self-serving they were. My brothers and I gave mom stuff that made our lives better—on our terms. Obeying Christ will make your life better too, but not necessarily on your terms. And that's the point. Christ has given us the terms for our expression of love: to obey his commands and follow his teachings.

Let's look at some of those commands and teachings. You may be surprised by what you find.

If You Love Me, You'll Obey Me

Questions to Ponder

1. Mark shared his experience of feeling like an outsider during his trip to Sacramento. Have you ever felt like an outsider? If so, were you eventually able to fit in, or did you remain an outsider?

2. Have you ever wished you could just start over? If so, why? How would that make a difference?

3. Mark wanted to be more like Jesus, but he found it difficult to do when he returned home from Sacramento. Why is it hard to change who we are—even when we want to?

4. How do Jesus' words, "If you love me you'll obey me," make you feel? Is there an area of disobedience that you need to take care of? If so, what will you do?

5. By seeing to the physical needs of her guests, Martha was doing a good thing; but she missed the better thing that was right in front of her. What are some of the "good" things in life that keep us from the "better" things?

6. Are there some good things in your life right now that keep you from experiencing something better? If so, what can you do about it?

CHAPTER 4

AND THE AWARD FOR GREATEST COMMANDMENT GOES TO...

It's too bad shows like *Saturday Night Live* and *MADtv* didn't exist in Jesus' day. They would've had a field day making fun of the Pharisees, a group of Jewish religious scholars who had a tremendous influence on how the Jewish people viewed Scripture.

An odd mixture of bookworm and performance artist, the Pharisees were known for their showy displays of religious observance. They offered up elaborate, self-serving prayers in loud voices in public places. They made a ritual of meticulously washing their hands in order to demonstrate their purity. They engaged in debates over whether or not a hen was allowed to lay an egg on the Sabbath (no joke).

While it's easy to make fun of such over-the-top behavior, I'll be honest with you: the things I read about the Pharisees scare me. You see, those religious leaders were extremely smart. They *memorized* the first five books of the Old Testament, also known as the Law. (How many Bible verses do you know by heart?) And all their showiness aside, the Pharisees were genuinely concerned about living their beliefs—which, incidentally, were quite close to those of Jesus. Their desire to put into action what they read in Scripture led them to create a list of rules, called the Mishnah, to guide their everyday actions. (To call it a "list" is an understatement. At the time of Christ, the Mishnah was about 700 pages long.) Yet those learned men (no ladies allowed) who were so committed to obeying God's rules totally missed the fact that Jesus, the Messiah they'd all been looking for, had finally come to them.

So it scares me to think that while I may be adept at studying God's Word and applying it to my life, I may in fact have a blind spot that would cause me to miss Jesus if he were to walk up to me on the street (which, by the way, I don't anticipate will happen).

I should point out that not all of the Pharisees missed the arrival of the Messiah. Some, such as Nicodemus and Joseph of Arimathea, eventually became followers of Christ. However, the majority of the Pharisees felt threatened by Jesus' message—not to mention his popularity among the people. Several times the religious leaders tried either to trap Jesus with their logic or trick him into saying the wrong thing. But Jesus' Scripture-based answers were always perfect.

One day, after Jesus had silenced some argumentative Sadducees (another group of Jewish religious thinkers) with his astounding logic, the Pharisees sent a teacher of the law to test him. The teacher simply asked, "Which is the greatest commandment in the Law?" That may not seem like a trick

And the Award for Greatest Commandment Goes To…

question, but it was. After all, if all the laws were God-given, how could one be better than another? This law expert thought he'd asked a question that Jesus couldn't answer without hanging himself with his words.

But Jesus' response was straightforward and to the point: "Love the Lord your God with all your heart and with all your soul and with all your mind. This is the first and greatest commandment" (Matthew 22:37-38). Jesus quoted Deuteronomy 6:5 and then summarized the first tablet of the Ten Commandments. In doing so, not only did he silence the Pharisees (yet again), but he also gave us a vital clue as to how we can show our love for him.

Remember, Jesus also said, "If you love me, you will obey what I command" (John 14:15). Well, here is commandment number one: to love him with our entire selves—hearts, souls, and minds. Let's take a closer look at each of these three components.

Loving God with All Your Heart

The word *heart* is used figuratively to describe the center of our desire and passion. When Jesus says we should love him with our hearts, it's that desire and passion he's referring to. Most of us can probably recall times when we've had strong emotions of love for and devotion to God. If you've participated in church activities for much of your life, as I have, you've probably been to a special event like a camp or conference where you truly felt moved by God. Maybe you had your heart broken and shed some tears. Maybe you lifted your hands high as you sang songs of love and devotion to your Creator and Savior.

I remember attending a large men's conference at Texas Stadium, located a few minutes away from my new house in Dallas. I'd just moved in the day before and was running a bit late. As I walked through the parking lot, I could hear the voices of tens of thousands of men singing "How Great Thou Art." The sound of so many voices singing praise to God moved me in a profound way. Tears filled my eyes as I walked from my car to the stadium. I'd heard the song many times before in my church, but never in such a dramatic way. I felt deep emotion for God that day.

After the conference was over, I made the short trip back to my new home and found my wife in the midst of boxes and furniture, trying to get our belongings in order. Though I'd been incredibly high on emotion just a short time earlier, it took only a few hours of unpacking to lose the feelings I'd experienced.

Maybe you've had a similar experience. I get many e-mails from students who've attended our PlanetWisdom conferences asking, "How can I keep my feelings after these special events?" But before we can answer that question, we need to understand the heart better.

Let's see what Scripture says: "As water reflects a face, so a man's heart reflects the man" (Proverbs 27:19). If you were to ask my wife why she was attracted to me, she'd tell you that next to my handsome features (pause for laughter), what she was most interested in was my passion for know-

And the Award for Greatest Commandment Goes To...

ing and serving God. That passion—that desire—revealed the kind of person I was. Take a moment to think about the people you admire, or think about your friends. What are the passions and desires of their lives?

If the heart reveals who we truly are, then it makes sense that Jesus would want us to love God with all of it. In order to be a genuine follower of Christ, we need a desire and passion for him. The times when I feel distant from God are also typically the times when I become passionate about the wrong things and God is no longer the desire of my heart.

Jeremiah 17:9-10 says, "The heart is deceitful above all things and beyond cure. Who can understand it? I the Lord search the heart and examine the mind, to reward a man according to his conduct, according to what his deeds deserve."

The heart is a fickle thing. When I was in junior high, I fell in love with a girl. Being a rather devoted person, not prone to flinging my affections around, I'm pretty convinced I would have married her—if she hadn't dumped me six weeks later. When she called to break up (the phone is the coward's tool for ending relationships), I asked her why. She said she didn't really know; she just felt like she wanted to go out with another guy she'd met. Bottom line: she was boy crazy. Her heart changed with the wind. Our high school years would see her cycle through several boyfriends. I couldn't understand it; but then again, I can't understand my own feelings most of the time.

Let's do an experiment right now. For 10 seconds I want you to feel happy. Do it now and then meet me in the next paragraph.

Good. Thanks for coming back. Now for part two—I want you to feel sad for 10 seconds, and then I'll meet you in the next paragraph. Do it now—feel sad.

Don't continue reading until you've tried both parts of the experiment. If you're done, what happened? Did your feelings really change? You may have made different faces, either smiling or frowning, but my guess is your feelings didn't change. That's what makes feelings so fickle.

I feel as though you and I are getting to be friends here, so I'm going to let you in on a secret: I can't control my feelings either. There are lots of things I don't "feel" like doing. For instance, because I travel on weekends, I rarely "feel" like going to church when Sunday comes around. And since I'm being really honest with you, I'll even make this last confession: I hardly ever "feel" like reading my Bible. That puts me in an awkward position as a follower of Christ and as a minister, doesn't it? What good am I if I don't feel like going to church or reading my Bible?

If you haven't thrown down this book in disgust over my confession, I'll bet you can identify with my situation. There are probably lots of things you don't "feel" like doing either. You see, the heart is deceitful. We don't feel like doing the things we know we should do. And no matter what we try, we can't seem to "make" the feelings happen.

And the Award for Greatest Commandment Goes To...

What's even worse is that instead of having feelings for the things I know I should do—the things that are good for me—I often have feelings for things that aren't so good for me. So I find myself struggling with the desire to do destructive things in my life. Paul wrote about this struggle in Galatians 5:17: "For the sinful nature desires what is contrary to the Spirit, and the Spirit what is contrary to the sinful nature. They are in conflict with each other, so that you do not do what you want." (You'll find a similar description of Paul's struggle in Romans 7:15-25.)

That struggle raises an obvious question: Since I don't seem to have the ability to influence my emotions, how can I get myself going in the right direction? Christian psychiatrist Dr. Frank Minirth, a friend of mine, once told me that feelings often follow behavior. So if you want to influence your feelings, you have to do something even when you don't initially feel like it.

That strategy rings true in my own life. I may not feel like going to church, but I find that once I get off the couch and go, I really enjoy being there. Lots of times the church leaders leave me a set of church keys to lock up the place because I'm one of the last ones there! So when it comes to reading the Bible, I may not have the feelings to open it up, but once I do, I can hardly put it down.

I think a big part of our struggle to love God with all of our hearts is that we've become hooked on feelings, not realizing the heart is so much more. We're told romantic love is an emotional thing. While there is an emotional aspect to it, it isn't the deepest part of desire and passion. My wife and

I have been married for 13 years now. When we had our 10-year anniversary, we spent some time reflecting on our marriage. We laughed at how much we thought we were in love when we were newlyweds. We had some well-intentioned feelings and emotions about one another back then; but after 10 years, we've come to know the love of the heart on a much deeper and more powerful level.

That doesn't mean emotions aren't important. My wife wouldn't be very happy if I didn't have emotional feelings for her. It's just that we now realize there's much, much more to passion and desire. It's the same with God. He wants us to have emotional feelings toward him, but he wants our love to run on deeper levels too.

You may be frustrated by your relationship with God because you can't recapture the feelings you had at camp or a conference. If so, you need to remind yourself that those special feelings are not the kind of heart love that sustains a relationship. When it comes to your relationship with God, rather than allowing your feelings to drive your actions, try taking action and see what happens to your feelings.

Before we move on to the next section, let me ask you a few questions to get a sense of where your desires are right now. Be honest.

* What are you passionate about?

* How do you spend your time?

* What do you buy with your money?

And the Award for Greatest Commandment Goes To...

* What do you dream about doing when you have some free time?

* What are you willing to suffer for?

Based on your answers, would you say you love God with all of your heart?

Loving God with All Your Soul

The soul is the non-physical part of us—our immaterial self. It's also the motivating force or will in our lives. The soul is who we truly are. I wrote a book with Christian philosopher Dr. J.P. Moreland called *Smart Faith: Loving Your God with All Your Mind*. While working on that book, we discussed the nature of the soul. J.P. recounted a conversation he'd had with his daughter when she was young. She told him it would be easier to pray to God if he were in the room with them and in some physical form. J.P. replied, "You haven't seen God, but you haven't really seen me either. You see my body, but not my soul, my real self. That's invisible too." J.P. was trying to help his daughter understand that people are more than physical presences. That concept is interesting to me because we live in a culture that puts so much emphasis on our physical beings, yet rarely focuses on the invisible part of our selves.

I'll admit I'm a bit of a sucker for reality television shows. They're my guilty pleasure. One of the shows I got hooked on was called *The Swan*. Here's how it worked: the producers would select a couple of "ugly ducklings"—physically unattractive women—and put them through thousands of dollars of plastic surgery, diet and fitness programs, and even some counseling to help turn them into beautiful "swans." Obviously, the emphasis was on the women's physical transformations, although I do have to give the producers props for doing the counseling part too.

One episode featured a woman who was extremely bitter as a result of her relationship trouble with a guy. (I think he cheated on her.) She wanted to improve her image so she could "show him" by being attractive to other men. They put her through the program; and when she was revealed at the end, I had to admit, she looked much, *much* better. The doctors had done amazing work.

While they were able to change the woman's physical appearance, however, they could do nothing about what was going on inside of her. When the host interviewed her after the transformation, all that came out of her mouth was bitterness. She showed her soul—her true self—and it wasn't pretty. All the physical attractiveness she'd acquired was worthless because she had no inner beauty to support it. Her soul was damaged, but no surgeon can fix that.

So how do you know if your soul is in need of attention? How do you love God with your soul when it's invisible? Let's address the first question first. Do any of the following statements apply to you?

* You're physically fit, but often exhausted and tired.

* You have a hard time focusing on things.

And the Award for Greatest Commandment Goes To...

* You cannot fall asleep easily.

* You feel numb toward spiritual things; nothing about God excites you.

* You feel as though your life is shallow.

* You're easily distracted during church, school, or while reading because of a conversation in your head.

If any of those symptoms ring a bell with you, your soul may need attention and care. The problem we face in this life is something called "dualism." Dualism occurs when we separate the physical and spiritual parts of life. You may have heard the term "Sunday Christian" to describe someone who seems concerned about God at church and then does whatever he pleases during the remainder of the week.

Dualism is kind of like that, only it's much more intense. A dualistic person lives "dual" lives that never seem to connect. The music you listen to, the TV shows you watch, your job, your school activities, and the education you receive are all connected to your spiritual life. There is no way to separate them without damaging your soul. Yet many of us try to live in a dualistic way, keeping our spiritual life distinctly separate from everything else.

In the book *The Spiritual Life*, author Evelyn Underhill wrote this about dualism:

Most of our conflicts and difficulties come from trying to deal with the spiritual and practical aspects of our life separately instead of realizing them as parts of one whole. If our practical life is centered on our own interests; cluttered up by possessions; distracted by our ambitions, passions, wants and worries; beset by a sense of our own rights and importance, or anxiety for our own future or longings for our own success; we need not expect that our spiritual life will be a contrast to all this.

In other words, if you're having trouble with a boyfriend or girlfriend, your parents, money, or grades, you shouldn't be surprised that your spiritual life is in disarray too. Similarly, if your spiritual life is in order, there's a good chance the other areas of your life will be as well.

The challenge is to love God with one's whole self, including the true self—the soul. The reason why so many people don't have healthy souls is because they're afraid of losing something that Jesus says isn't worth having.

Then he called the crowd to him along with his disciples and said: "If anyone would come after me, he must deny himself and take up his cross and follow me. For whoever wants to save his life will lose it, but whoever loses his life for me and for the gospel will save it. What good is it for a man to gain the whole world, yet forfeit his soul? Or what can a man give in exchange for his soul?" (Mark 8:34-37)

The way to care for this part of us, which can't be seen in a mirror or fixed with a diet program or plastic surgery, involves three basic routines. I've found the practice of these routines is what my soul needs.

And the Award for Greatest Commandment Goes To...

Silence and Solitude

Life in our culture is noisy. Most of us wake up to an alarm, turn on music while we get ready for the day, go to the car where more music is playing, and then go to school or work where noise is abundant. Those who are lucky enough to have their own room can sometimes find solitude, but many of us don't have that luxury. And that's a problem.

One thing we know about Jesus, which I find fascinating, is that he routinely found ways to be alone. Even though he spent only a short time on earth, he continually looked for silence and solitude, even when it meant leaving people who were looking for him. Luke 5:15-16 says, "Yet the news about him spread all the more, so that crowds of people came to hear him and to be healed of their sicknesses. But Jesus often withdrew to lonely places and prayed." And Mark 1:35-37 says, "Very early in the morning, while it was still dark, Jesus got up, left the house and went off to a solitary place, where he prayed. Simon and his companions went to look for him, and when they found him, they exclaimed: 'Everyone is looking for you!'"

Why did Jesus place such a priority on solitude? Remember, he was 100 percent human and 100 percent God. Perhaps his self-imposed periods of silence helped him keep the tension between these two realities in their proper place.

In his book *The Way of the Heart*, author Henri Nouwen describes the benefits of solitude:

In solitude I get rid of my scaffolding: no friends to talk with, no telephone calls to make, no meetings to attend, no music to entertain, no books to distract, just me—naked, vulnerable, weak, sinful, depraved, broken—nothing. It is this nothingness that I have to face in my solitude, a nothingness so dreadful that everything in me wants to run to my friends, my work, and my distractions so that I can forget my nothingness and make myself believe that I am worth something...That is the struggle. It is the struggle to die to the false self.

Perhaps the fallen world around us causes us to create a false self that desires to keep us from living as our true self. If so, times of silence and solitude give us opportunity to put matters of self into proper perspective.

Maybe that's what happened in John 6:14-15:

After the people saw the miraculous sign that Jesus did, they began to say, "Surely this is the Prophet who is to come into the world." Jesus, knowing that they intended to come and make him king by force, withdrew again to a mountain by himself.

Jesus' followers wanted to make Jesus something he wasn't. They wanted to crown him king on their terms. While Jesus *is* King of kings, his earthly purpose was to go to the cross, which was about 180 degrees from what his followers had in mind. To keep his focus clear, Jesus separated himself from the world.

The world you live in is trying to pull you away from your obedience and love for God. That pull may come in many attractive forms, but we must not be swayed. Our purpose

And the Award for Greatest Commandment Goes To...

is to do what God wants. Regular intervals of silence and solitude can help us achieve that purpose.

PRAYER

The movie *Saved!* is a satire of life in a Christian school. In one scene the lead character, Mary (played by Jena Malone), realizes she's totally screwed everything up and everything around her is falling apart. Standing in front of a larger-than-life portrait of Jesus, Mary looks at the painting as though she's going to pray, then unleashes a series of profanities. My friend Mike told me that was one of the most honest prayers he'd ever heard.

While the movie made me think about the stupid un-Christlike things we do as Christians, Mike's comment got me thinking. *Was that an honest prayer?* I realize many people pray using words they can't honestly say. In the movie, Mary had nothing good to say—only that life was really messed up. How often do we fail to be honest in our prayers to God? I enjoy reading the Psalms in Eugene Peterson's *The Message* because he really captured the emotion David was experiencing when he cried out to God. David was honest in his prayers. And in his honesty, he found hope in the Lord.

Most people I know very rarely talk to God, and that's a shame. I've found that sharing the highs and lows of my life with him soothes my soul. As I make my requests and thanks known to him, I'm constantly aware that he is God and I am not.

We know Jesus prayed a lot, especially when he was alone. And when he taught about prayer, he pretty much condemned people who were putting on a show with their words:

And when you pray, do not be like the hypocrites, for they love to pray standing in the synagogues and on the street corners to be seen by men. I tell you the truth, they have received their reward in full. But when you pray, go into your room, close the door and pray to your Father, who is unseen. Then your Father, who sees what is done in secret, will reward you. And when you pray, do not keep on babbling like pagans, for they think they will be heard because of their many words. Do not be like them, for your Father knows what you need before you ask him. (Matthew 6:5-9)

How many people do you know who change their voice and vocabulary when they pray out loud? You know what I'm talking about, don't you? They speak in a Shakespearean voice and use ancient words. Do you ever get the feeling they're trying to impress you (and everyone else in the room) with their prayers?

Several years ago we had an online prayer gathering at our Web site, www.PlanetWisdom.com. We called the event Standing in the Gap. People signed up to pray every half hour, 24 hours a day, for an entire week. We set up a chat room so people could type their prayers and pray with anyone who was logged on. Many students said it was the best prayer time they'd ever experienced. I asked why and many said they usually have a hard time praying silently because

And the Award for Greatest Commandment Goes To...

they fall asleep. But praying in the chat room kept them alert as they wrote their prayers. Maybe that could help you too. Try praying aloud or writing out your prayers as David did in the Psalms.

SIMPLICITY

Jesus was a simple guy. He had just a few close friends, lived on very little money, and owned only one piece of clothing when he died—which, by the way, was the only personal possession of his that the Bible mentions. How does that compare with life in our material culture?

In the United States we rent storage units to hold all the stuff we don't use, but don't want to get rid of. And all the while, our culture tells us we need more and more. So we spend most of our lives trying to get stuff that really isn't all that meaningful.

All of our stuff—and our perceived lack of stuff—causes stress on the soul. Our stuff also serves to distract us from being who God calls us to be. Look around your room. Take a peek at your calendar. Consider your plans for the future. How much of it involves simplifying your life and how much involves complicating it? God desires us to be diligent and to work hard, but he also wants our souls to be uncluttered. His way of living is much less hurried and hectic.

Jesus said, "Come to me, all you who are weary and burdened, and I will give you rest. Take my yoke upon you and learn from me, for I am gentle and humble in heart, and you will find rest for your souls. For my yoke is easy and my burden is light" (Matthew 11:28-30).

Loving God with All Your Mind

Of all the components of our lives, the mind is probably the most neglected when it comes to showing our love for God. Many people believe following Christ is a matter of faith and faith has nothing to do with intellect. But Christ never asks us to give up our ability to think and reason. In fact Peter, one of Jesus' disciples, wrote that every Christian should "Always be prepared to give an answer to everyone who asks you to give the reason for the hope that you have. But do this with gentleness and respect" (1 Peter 3:15).

What reason would you give for putting your hope in Jesus? Would it stand up to scrutiny? It's important to remember that Peter was not a scholar or an intellectual; he was a fisherman. Yet he believed the ability to reason was essential to our faith.

In Romans 12:2 Paul writes that we should be transformed by the renewing of our minds. In other words, there's a time to put away the puppet show Bible stories and Veggie Tales DVDs and go deeper into our understanding of Christ. A lack of the kind of transformation Paul's talking about may be the reason why so many young adults fall away from Christianity when they go to college. Beliefs are the rails upon which our lives run. We almost always act according to what we *really* believe. That's why behavior is a good indica-

And the Award for Greatest Commandment Goes To...

tor of what a person's beliefs are. The lack of a strong mind can make Christianity appear very weak indeed.

As I mentioned earlier, I've written an entire book on this subject with Dr. J.P. Moreland. It's called *Smart Faith* (NavPress, 2005), and in it we discuss the basis of what makes a belief. Allow me to paraphrase some of our conclusions:

CONTENT

The content of a belief determines "what" we believe. The content may include what we believe about God, morality, politics, life after death, and so on. The content shapes our lives and our actions. One's beliefs are so important that, according to Scripture, our eternal destiny is determined by what we believe about Jesus Christ.

It seems that most people today are inclined to think that the sincerity or fervency of their beliefs are more important than their content. If I believe that grape jelly will fuel my car better than gasoline, I can believe it as strongly as I want but the car isn't going anywhere. Reality doesn't care how fervently we believe something. What matters is not whether I strongly believe, but whether what I believe is true or not.

I've had friends tell me they live basically good lives and they don't believe God will really allow anyone to go to hell. They can believe this all they want to, but the Bible is clear that there is a punishment for sin, and that

Christ is the only way to find life and escape that punishment. No matter how much they believe this, if the content is not true, it isn't worth believing. But content will shape your life whether it is true or not.

STRENGTH

There is more to a belief than its content, however. Many students know how to give the right answer at church, but the real question is how strongly they believe it. To have strength of conviction you have to be at least more than 50 percent convinced that it is true. If it were fifty-fifty, you wouldn't have the belief in question. Instead you would still be in the process of deciding whether you believed or not. As you gain evidence and support for a belief, its strength grows for you. It may start off as plausible then become fairly likely, quite likely, beyond reasonable doubt, or complete certainty.

For most of my life I've had no problem believing Jesus rose from the dead. I never questioned this important aspect of my faith. Incredibly, I managed to go through most of my life, even graduating from college, without anyone ever challenging my belief that Jesus actually rose from the dead. That said, I was preparing a message on the resurrection of Christ and I began to read books written by people who'd examined the resurrection of Christ in depth. Although I have always believed this without question, I was amazed at the incredible reasonable and rational evidence for the resurrection of Christ! I quickly realized a transformation in my life

And the Award for Greatest Commandment Goes To...

as the strength of my belief increased. I never would have characterized my belief as weak, but I found a new confidence and boldness in my faith, life, and ministry after this learning took place. The more you are certain of a belief, the more it becomes a part of your very soul, and the more you rely on it as a basis for action.

Centrality

This idea may be less common than the other two, but centrality is easily grasped. The centrality of a belief is the degree of importance the belief plays in your entire set of beliefs, that is, in your worldview. The more central a belief is, the greater the impact it makes in your daily life. I believe exercise is good for you. In fact I have seen evidence that consistent exercise will benefit the heart and body greatly. So I even believe strongly that exercise is good for you. So you might find me exercising, right? Nope. At this time in my life, even though I have true content and strength in the belief, exercise is not a central belief in my life. Now I may become ill or have a situation arise that moves exercise to the center of my life, but for now, this isn't a central belief in my life. My belief in God, Jesus Christ, and absolute morality are very central to my life, more central now than when I first trusted Christ for salvation.

For many Christians, they hold true beliefs about God, but they are not central to their lives and so they have very little impact on how they live each day.

Plausibility

Many great movies are based on convincing the viewer of the plausibility of the central concept for the story. For instance *Jurassic Park* would not have been a success (even with the amazing special effects and computer generated dinosaurs) unless they could convince the viewer that dinosaurs could actually be genetically engineered. Seeing is not merely believing; the storyteller had to create a world where we could believe this incredible thing could possibly happen. My dad was always a "fantasy killer" at the movies because he could never buy in to the artificial and unrealistic world that was being pushed on the audience. He continually pointed out the credibility gaps in the story and plot structure. To be believable, an idea has to be plausible.

If a friend approached you with the idea that the earth is actually flat, you would not even entertain such a notion. Our culture and society have so much accepted the concept that the earth is round that any argument regarding a flat earth seems ridiculous and laughable.

Consider the issue of racism in our culture as it relates to African Americans. Any honest examination of slavery in America will find it to be a despicable and inhumane practice. It is hard to imagine that people could treat other humans in such a manner that was in direct contrast from the very American beliefs of individual freedom and liberty. But we must understand the plausibility structure of the world in that era. Slaves were not seen as human beings, the plausibility of these slaves having equal rights was not part of their plausibility structure, until many thinking and thoughtful people began to realize the incongruities. Through much difficulty and a civil war, slavery ended in our country.

But plausibility structures do not change overnight. The ability of many Americans to perceive a person of darker skin as an equal was simply not plausible. It has taken generations to make the progress we now see in our country because it has taken time for people to change the way they think about people of other ethnic backgrounds.

So beliefs have to be plausible to be credible. This is a great challenge for many of the Christian beliefs we hold true in America today. There was a time in American culture when a belief in God and the authority of the Scriptures was considered plausible within American values and beliefs. In 1925 when creation and evolution were put on trial in the Scopes Monkey trial, we saw the beginning of the rapid decline in the plausibility of Christian ideas in American society. Already the Christian mind had been weakened, so much so that conservative Christianity was considered an embarrassment and was dismissed by cultural movers and shakers following the Scopes trial. Christianity was not what should have been viewed as embarrassing, rather the lack of intellect portrayed by Christians, as they were unable to defend their faith using reasonable arguments. As a result, we now live in the most secular culture in all of history.

If a culture reaches a point where the beliefs of Christianity are no longer part of its plausibility structure, fewer and fewer people will be able to entertain the idea that the idea is even true.

So the transformation of the mind requires more than merely the discovery of the right beliefs. One must also be able to back up and support those beliefs, developing a strength of conviction. Finally we must bring the right beliefs to the center of our lives where they make an impact on our daily lives.

When we love God with everything we are, we can be confident we're doing what he wants us to do. But that's not all he wants. Our love for God focuses on our vertical relationship with him. However, he is also concerned about our horizontal relationships with other people. Which brings us to the second greatest commandment, according to Jesus.

Questions to Ponder

1. Have you ever seen anyone act like a Pharisee? If so, how?

2. If you'd been one of the Pharisees, do you think it would've been difficult for you to believe in Jesus? Why or why not?

3. Why do you think Jesus considered the command to love God with all your heart, soul, and mind to be the greatest

And the Award for Greatest Commandment Goes To...

commandment? How difficult is that command to actually live out in your life? Why?

4. What are you passionate about? How do you spend your time? What do you spend your money on? What do you dream of doing in your free time? What are you willing to suffer for?

5. What would it take for you to love God with all your heart?

6. If someone asked you for a reason for the hope you have in Christ, what would you tell him?

7. What shape is your soul in? Have you spent time in prayer, silence, and solitude lately? Do you think it would help you? Why or why not?

8. How can you simplify your life?

CHAPTER 5

YOU DIDN'T ASK FOR NUMBER TWO, BUT I'LL GIVE IT TO YOU ANYWAY

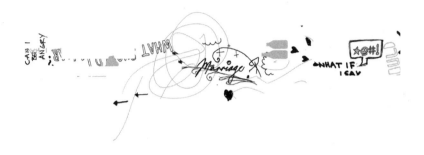

Jesus' words continue to haunt me: "If you love me, you will obey what I command." He gave us a great starting point when he told the Pharisees the greatest commandment was to love God with our hearts, souls, and minds. (And in the process, he gave the Pharisees little to challenge him on.)

But Jesus didn't stop there. He offered up the second greatest command as well: "And the second is like it: 'Love your neighbor as yourself.' All the Law and the Prophets hang on these two commandments" (Matthew 22:39-40). Jesus wants us to know that while our love for God is important, our love for people is important too.

I've shared some personal stories about growing up as a Christian. Some of them I'm not terribly proud of. The things I'm most embarrassed about have to do with the way I treated people. It's not that I was terrible to others; it's that I didn't go out of my way to love them. That's where a lot of us make a mistake. We think the opposite of love is hate, but it's not. The opposite of love is indifference, simply lacking interest in a person.

Loving Enemies

Most of my life I never really "hated" anyone. I was considered a friendly person. I had enough rapport with my peers to win every election I entered for class president, from seventh grade through my senior year of high school. So I thought I was doing a pretty good job of relating to other people. Like many Christians, I believed that as long as I didn't "hate" anyone, then I was succeeding in loving others. But the reality was very different. I was actually so proud and so arrogant that I didn't really care about many other people. I lived as though I were the only person in the world who mattered.

Maybe that's why Jesus' teaching about loving others seemed so revolutionary to me. Take a look at what he says in Luke 6:27-28: "But I tell you who hear me: Love your enemies, do good to those who hate you, bless those who curse you, pray for those who mistreat you." Do you see the action that a "Jesus kind of love" requires? He doesn't tell us to ignore the people we don't like—he tells us to do good to them.

I can't think of anyone in my life I would actually label an enemy. There certainly have been people I didn't care for, as well as people who didn't really like me. But I wouldn't put them in the "enemy" category. What about you? Are there people in your life whom you'd consider to be your enemies? Whether you label them full-fledged foes or people you don't like a whole lot, I think the teaching applies.

Jesus wants us to engage our enemies in loving ways. That might involve something as simple as presenting them with a birthday card with a special note inside. (Don't know when their birthday is? Find out!) Or maybe it means including them whenever you give out Valentine's Day goodies or Christmas cards. Perhaps you pick them to be on your team in P.E. I'm not a very good athlete, so I was usually picked last whenever teams were chosen. That's why it always meant a lot to me when someone would pick me before the other students he knew to be better players.

To be honest, it's difficult to make a list of every possible way to "do good" to enemies because different people will find themselves in different situations with different opportunities. The key is to do something—anything—that will benefit the person, rather than do nothing at all.

Even When It's Inconvenient

Maybe there are people you work hard to avoid in your everyday life. You know their class schedules and you navigate the halls in such a way that you never encounter them. Those are the people you're supposed to love—and not just in theory. Jesus instructs his followers to go out of their way to *show* love to people.

When was the last time someone yelled at you or made fun of you? How did you react? According to Jesus, rather than responding in kind, his followers have a responsibility to bless those who wrong us. When I was in college, there was a guy who really didn't like me very much. What's more, I knew he was saying untrue and hateful things about me behind my back. What did I do? I went out of my way to be near him whenever possible, and I looked for ways to encourage him and praise him for the things he was doing well. I'm sure it drove him nuts, but I didn't do it to be clever or cute or to "fake" being a good guy. I could tell he was a bitter person, and I was concerned for him.

Not only are we to go out of our way to do good to our enemies, but we're also expected to pray for them. (To be honest, I sometimes neglect to pray for people I like a whole bunch. Taking time to pray for people who mistreat me? That requires a new way of thinking.)

I've heard stories about mothers and wives going to prison to pray with and for the person who murdered their sons or husbands. Those are truly remarkable acts of love and forgiveness. But I think it might be easier for me to do that than to pray for some of the people I see every day who just annoy me. Here's why I say that. When someone really wrongs me, it actually helps me to be able to forgive him for what he's done. I sense relief and closure when I reach that point, no matter how difficult it is to come to. Typically, the really big things (like a major betrayal of trust, stealing, or murder) are extreme cases that happen only once or twice. It's the repeat offenders in smaller areas of life (like talking too much or being negative all the time or sporting an "I'm all that" attitude) that get on my nerves every day and make it harder for me to love someone.

You Didn't Ask for Number Two, but I'll Give It to You Anyway

As we continue to read Jesus' teaching in Luke 6:29-33, we see just how much he asks of us:

> If someone strikes you on one cheek, turn to him the other also. If someone takes your cloak, do not stop him from taking your tunic. Give to everyone who asks you, and if anyone takes what belongs to you, do not demand it back. Do to others as you would have them do to you. If you love those who love you, what credit is that to you? Even "sinners" love those who love them. And if you do good to those who are good to you, what credit is that to you? Even "sinners" do that.

Jesus wants our love to stand out, to be remarkable. He wants us to exceed the norm. Imagine having someone take a swing at you and instead of fighting back, you make yourself vulnerable to another punch. It might hurt—but it certainly would get the attention of the person taking the swing.

Have you ever seen the movie *Big Fish*? In one scene the hero, Edward Bloom (played by Ewan McGregor), gets in a fight with the fiancé of the girl he's certain he's supposed to marry. The girl begs Edward not to hurt the guy, so he gives his word that he won't touch her fiancé. What happens next is painful to watch. The fiancé absolutely whales on Edward, who does nothing but take it. In the end, Edward gets the girl because she sees the strength of his character. Similarly, our love for God often requires us to do unusual things—such as going beyond the call of duty.

Jesus says when people ask you for something, your best response is to look for ways to give them more. I remember telling Rick Knight, a man at my church, that I really loved his tie. He took it off right there and gave it to me! I was blown away! The next time your parents ask you to do something, do it quickly and then come back (rather than running and hiding) and ask them if there's anything else you can do for them. You'll blow them away! When your brother or sister wants to change the channel, hand over the remote and ask them if you can get them something to drink while they watch. You'll blow them away! Get in the habit of thinking about not only what people ask of you, but also what you can do as a bonus because you want to. It's more difficult than you might think.

Jesus also encourages us to give without expecting anything in return. The weight of an unpaid debt is a relationship killer. I had a friend borrow my red zippered jacket that was similar to the one Michael Jackson wore in his "Beat It" video. I didn't wear it seriously, only as a joke. But my friend could do all the Michael Jackson moves, so it was really funny when he wore the jacket and pretended to be Michael. One day he borrowed the jacket to entertain friends at his high school, and I never got it back. For weeks, this friend avoided me and made up excuses about the jacket. I could tell he'd either lost it or it had been stolen, but he was too afraid to be honest with me.

Losing a jacket was one thing, but losing a friend is a much bigger loss. I've learned that when I loan something to someone, I should consider it gone. I never want a possession to take the place of a friendship.

You Didn't Ask for Number Two, but I'll Give It to You Anyway

Excuses, Excuses

So what are some of our excuses for not being more generous toward others? See if these three are familiar:

1) **I'm helping by not helping.** When it comes to giving, we sometimes fool ourselves into thinking we're helping by not doing anything at all. When we see the man at the corner with the "Will work for food" sign, we think, *I'll bet he just wants money for drugs or alcohol. So I'm really helping him by not giving him any money.*

2) **People are happier in poverty.** I get upset when short-term missionaries return from their trip and say something like, "These people have so much less than we do, yet they're so happy—way happier than most Americans I know." Do we really believe they're happier in poverty? Or is it just a way for us not to feel guilty for all the stuff we have? You see, real love gives generously and asks nothing in return.

3) **I don't have much to give.** Jesus observed a woman giving two mites as an offering (pull a handful of pennies out of your pocket and you'll have roughly the equivalent of one mite) and a rich man giving the equivalent of thousands of dollars. Jesus asked, "Who is giving more?" The answer was the woman because it was literally all she had. The rich man was giving only a fraction of his wealth. The lesson is this—no matter your situation, you have something to offer until you have nothing at all.

Those are just a few reasons why people don't give generously. What's your excuse?

WHAT DOES GOD WANT FROM ME?

Look at what Jesus said at the end of the following passage in Luke: "But love your enemies, do good to them, and lend to them without expecting to get anything back. Then your reward will be great, and you will be sons of the Most High, because he is kind to the ungrateful and wicked. Be merciful, just as your Father is merciful" (Luke 6:35-36). It's a great motivation to be generous!

Great is the reward from God for those who do good and give generously with no strings attached.

Questions to Ponder

1. On a scale of one to ten, how good are you at loving people?

2. Do you consider anyone to be your enemy? If not, do you strongly dislike any of the people in your life? If so, why?

3. How do you act around those people?

4. What steps do you need to take in order to obey Jesus' command to love your enemies?

5. What is one way you could show God's amazing love to someone tomorrow?

You Didn't Ask for Number Two, but I'll Give It to You Anyway

CHAPTER 6

WHAT DOES IT LOOK LIKE TO "DO JUSTICE"?

In high school my friend Sarah forgot her history book all the time. I had history the period after her, so she often asked to borrow my book so she wouldn't be graded down for not bringing hers. Sarah was a Christian, but she wasn't nearly as committed to God as I was. That was obvious by the friends she hung out with and by certain "poor" choices she made. She also didn't go to church very regularly; and when she did go, it wasn't to the same one I attended. (This is my subtle way of telling you I was a better Christian than she was. Maybe you see where this is heading.) But hey—she was a sister in Christ, so she was cool with me.

One day she turned the corner after history class and we did the "history book handoff" as she went on to English. I sat down at my desk a few minutes before the bell rang; and when I opened my book, a note fell out. And that created a dilemma. I knew the note was Sarah's personal property. But she left it in my book—which technically, at least for the current semester, was *my* property. So I did what any honest

and decent individual would do after finding a secret note:
I read it.

It was the kind of letter where two people write and
they pass it back and forth during class—kind of like text
messaging, but with pen and paper. The note was between
Sarah and someone with the initials MB.

After reading just the first paragraph, I knew the letter was juicy because it was about a boy and it contained
details. Graphic details. I'd never seen pornography before,
so reading MB's note was the closest I'd ever come to the act
of sex before marriage.

I really wanted to know who "MB" was. I racked my
brain, but couldn't think of anyone with those initials. I had
to find out. I decided my best bet was to sneak a peek at
Mr. Richards' attendance record for third period—no easy
task. Mr. Richards was a cool guy, but he was also rather
secretive about his attendance sheet. (He wrote personal
comments and other private information about his students
there.) He typically took out the sheet during attendance
and then immediately returned it to a locked desk drawer.
However, sometimes he'd use it to record students' points
while the class played history trivia games. So I watched for
my chance all period long, but to no avail; the record was
never in a place where I could see it.

The next day Sarah asked if she could borrow my book
again. When she did the return handoff later that day, I
hurried to my desk to open the book. Sure enough, another
note fell out. It was also between Sarah and MB, but the

What Does It Look Like to "Do Justice"?

writing was scratchier, more frantic, and with sharp angles. It was obvious that a lot of emotion was poured into those two sheets of paper!

Feeling a little guilty and not wanting to draw attention to the fact that I was invading someone's privacy, I decided to read the note another time. I folded it up and put it in my back pocket.

I couldn't keep my eyes off the clock that period. I felt desperate for the class to end. I had to read the letter! I toyed with the idea of asking for a bathroom pass—something I seldom did. The teachers at my school had a way of humiliating students who asked to use the bathroom during class time. For instance, Mr. Richards made you carry an obnoxiously large toilet seat—his custom hall pass.

What's more, I hated the idea of everyone knowing where I was going and what I was going to do. In this case, given the fact that I was planning to read a long letter, I could imagine what people would say: "Man, he was gone for a long time!" or "Mark hardly ever uses the can, but when he does—watch out!" or "If it's that bad, why didn't he just stay home today?" I didn't need that, so I decided I'd wait until lunch to read the note.

I quickly grabbed my daily lunch purchase from the cafeteria (pepperoni French bread pizza and a carton of chocolate milk) and sat down. Some of my Christian friends sat at the table with me. One of them even started talking about honesty and right and wrong. I just smiled and kept eating my pizza.

WHAT DOES GOD WANT FROM ME?

Then it happened. Sarah walked up to me and asked if she could see my history book. "But history is over," I said, knowing exactly what she was after.

"Mark, just let me see the book," she replied. "I think I left something in there."

I was glad the letter was in my back pocket, but I still felt as though I were about to get caught. What if she saw the edge of the note sticking out? What would I do then?

Sarah flipped through the book and looked at me. "Where is it?"

"What?" I asked, feigning ignorance. "What are you looking for?"

"I left a note in here and it's important that it doesn't get read by the wrong person," she explained.

The note was getting warm in my back pocket, heating up as the conversation continued. I wanted to give it to her, but now I just *had* to know what it said. "I'm sorry, I didn't read any note in there today," I said.

Technically, I didn't lie. I didn't say I'd never seen the note; I said I hadn't *read* the note that may have been in the book that day (so that let me off the hook for the day before as well). I could feel the note tingling, as though it were going to jump right out of my back pocket and do a dance on the table in front of us, screaming, "He knows! He knows! He's a filthy liar!"

What Does It Look Like to "Do Justice"?

Sarah walked away, headed for Mr. Richards' room to search for a treasure she'd never find—unless she saw that giant red X painted on the seat of my pants.

When I got home that afternoon, I locked myself in the bathroom (since my bedroom had no door) and read the note. I wasn't prepared for what it said. MB was pregnant. What's more, she was considering getting an abortion at the end of the week.

I was sad for MB, but I was also ticked off at Sarah because she didn't come down harder on MB for getting pregnant in the first place. And instead of trying to convince her to reconsider the abortion, Sarah just told her to think things through before doing anything. Sarah also told MB that she'd love her no matter what MB did. How could Sarah do that? If MB had the abortion, she'd be a murderer! Then "MB" would also stand for "Murdered Baby"! MB was going to kill an innocent child just because she'd decided to act slutty with some guy. I had no compassion for her. And now I *really* wanted to know who MB was. While I was certain she wasn't the kind of girl I'd ever date, I wanted to be able to warn others about her.

The next day in English class, I had a breakthrough. When I entered the classroom, Shelly, a girl in our Christian club, was talking to the teacher, Ms. Patsy. I could tell Shelly was upset and barely holding back her tears as she talked. Then the bell rang and as Shelly headed for the door, Ms. Patsy asked her if she needed a pass to explain her tardiness to Mr. Prior.

Then it clicked. Shelly was in third period history. Her last name was Brown. And the name "Shelly" was short for "Michelle." I'd just found MB, and I was blown away. A quick check of the seating chart confirmed that Shelly sat near Sarah in third period history. What's more, Shelly didn't come to school for several days after that. She'd apparently done the deed. But I knew her secret, and I hated the fact that it seemed she'd gotten away with the whole thing and her life would go on as normal—without any consequences.

I wondered if perhaps I was meant to be God's tool for bringing justice to Shelly's life. I saved the letter, thinking one day I'd either mail it to her or leave it on her desk with a note that simply said, "I know!"—and no signature. Or even better, I'd wait until her wedding day, show up at the ceremony, and then pull out the letter. Yep, I *really* thought about doing those things. I was a wicked Christian. What's worse, I actually believed I'd somehow be *helping* God by doing those things!

Right and Wrong

If I'd followed through on my plans, I wouldn't have been the first Christian in history to do the wrong thing in the name of God. It seems everywhere you turn in the Bible, God's followers are being scolded for not doing the right things. The people of Israel were sent to the desert for 40 years because they didn't trust God to deliver them from the hands of the people who occupied the Promised Land. Moses was forbidden to enter the land God promised to the Israelites because he did the wrong thing. King David

What Does It Look Like to "Do Justice"?

committed adultery and plotted a murder. And when the apostle Peter once tried to correct Jesus, Jesus called him Satan (Matthew 16:22-23).

If you don't have a close relationship with God, it's easy to become confused about what he wants. You may do what you think is right, only to find out how wrong you were.

In the sixth chapter of Micah, God asks what he's done to burden the people of Israel. After all, he's the one who brought them out of slavery in Egypt. In response, Micah assumes the voice of the Israelites, asking what God wants from them. In a dramatic tone, Micah asks if he should give God calves and thousands of rams or maybe rivers of oil. Micah even goes so far as to ask if God wants the Israelites' firstborn children. Of course, Micah knew God didn't want human sacrifice; he was just showing the Israelites that God desires an inner spirit of worship, not an outward ritual.

In verse 8 Micah describes what God wants: "He has showed you, O man, what is good. And what does the Lord require of you? To act justly and to love mercy and to walk humbly with your God." The people of Israel already knew what God wanted, however, and Micah's words were not new to them. In fact, they recall several passages that were given to Israel in the past (Deuteronomy 10:12-13; Jeremiah 22:3; Isaiah 1:17).

So what does it look like to "act justly" and "love mercy"? I have a hunch it looks nothing like my actions and thoughts concerning MB's note.

WHAT DOES GOD WANT FROM ME?

The Struggle for Justice

The reason why many of us struggle with acting justly is because we have a warped perspective of how justice works. Even though America has one of the best justice systems in the world, it's far from perfect. We're continually reminded that some guilty people get away without punishment and some innocent people are punished for crimes they didn't commit.

Maybe that's why TV shows like *C.S.I.* are so popular. In those programs, cases are solved scientifically—and irrefutably. The evidence doesn't lie. The bad guys are caught at the end of the show, and we never have to watch the case go to trial where a hotshot defense attorney gets the perpetrator freed on a technicality, or where a jury is wooed into letting a guilty person walk.

Do you ever wonder why we care so much about right and wrong? It has to do with the reality that God is the ultimate judge. He is right in all he does, and he is fair in all his judgments. Because we're made in God's likeness, deep inside we all know there are things that are right and things that are wrong. Yet we struggle to exercise justice because we're all flawed. So how can we hold each other accountable?

It's a frustration we experience constantly: we want justice, but not for the things *we've* done. The sense of right and wrong that God's placed in each of us is a double-edged sword. The justice we long for is the very thing that shows us we're also guilty of sin.

What Does It Look Like to "Do Justice"?

How can we understand justice the way God wants us to? Repeat after me:

There is a Judge and I am not him!

Judge Not?

Proverbs 16:2 says, "All a man's ways seem innocent to him, but motives are weighed by the Lord." Justice is more than knowing right and wrong; it also involves weighing circumstances and issuing punishment or reward. While God grants nations permission to punish wrongdoers for the sake of society, he makes it clear that ultimate judgment comes from him alone. God assures us that everything judged as wicked will be punished (Proverbs 11:21), so we don't need to be concerned about such things.

What God asks is that we "do" justice—in other words, he wants us to act in a right manner toward other people. But the fact that we live in an imperfect world surrounded by imperfect people presents a challenge for us. People do things we don't agree with—things that offend us, things that violate our beliefs. Their actions call for a response on our part—a judgment of sorts.

But how can we pass judgment on someone without putting ourselves in God's place? The Bible suggests the key is motive—our ultimate goal in passing judgment. Look at the apostle Paul's words to the believers in Corinth:

It is actually reported that there is sexual immorality among you, and of a kind that does not occur even among pagans: A man has his father's wife. And you are proud! Shouldn't you rather have been filled with grief and have put out of your fellowship the man who did this? Even though I am not physically present, I am with you in spirit. And I have already passed judgment on the one who did this, just as if I were present. When you are assembled in the name of our Lord Jesus and I am with you in spirit, and the power of our Lord Jesus is present, hand this man over to Satan, so that the sinful nature may be destroyed and his spirit saved on the day of the Lord. (1 Corinthians 5:1-5)

You think you have problems in your church? In Corinth a man was having sex with his father's wife (we assume it wasn't his mother)! Notice that the other Christians in Corinth didn't seem bothered by the man's actions. Maybe they were happy to welcome him to the church and saw their tolerance of his actions as evidence of their kindness and acceptance. Paul, however, was not pleased that they refused to address the problem. His attitude suggests that it's okay to be troubled by the actions of others—especially when those actions have an impact on the health of the church.

Notice also that the woman involved in this sexual immorality isn't singled out for judgment. Apparently she wasn't part of the church community. That would suggest that we're to judge fellow Christians differently from unbelievers. (We'll talk more about that later in the chapter.)

What Does It Look Like to "Do Justice"?

But we really need to pay attention to the reason why Paul wants to kick the man out of the church. It was not to punish the man because punishment is for the Lord to hand out as he sees appropriate. Neither was the goal to humiliate the man or alienate him. Instead, Paul wanted to reconcile him to God and to the church. So we see that in doing justice our goal should be reconciliation—helping a person restore a good relationship with God and with others.

I know what some of you are thinking: *Isn't there a passage in the Bible that tells us not to judge?* Let's take a look at Jesus' words in Matthew's gospel:

> Do not judge, or you too will be judged. For in the same way you judge others, you will be judged, and with the measure you use, it will be measured to you. Why do you look at the speck of sawdust in your brother's eye and pay no attention to the plank in your own eye? How can you say to your brother, "Let me take the speck out of your eye," when all the time there is a plank in your own eye? You hypocrite, first take the plank out of your own eye, and then you will see clearly to remove the speck from your brother's eye. Do not give dogs what is sacred; do not throw your pearls to pigs. If you do, they may trample them under their feet, and then turn and tear you to pieces. (Matthew 7:1-6)

If you read the passage carefully, you'll see that it doesn't tell us we cannot judge; it tells us we must judge in a right manner.

Jesus wanted us to know that when we judge others, we'll be judged in the same way. Therefore, we need to make sure our hearts are right with God before we pass judgment on someone else. When we approach people about their sin, we need to make sure our motive is not to punish, humiliate, or alienate them. And if we're struggling with our own sin, it's difficult to help a brother or sister who's also struggling. It opens us up to charges of hypocrisy. So as we do justice—as we attempt to reconcile people to God—we must have a pure heart and life.

Before we move on, take a look at Jesus' comments about throwing pearls to pigs. What did he mean by that? Many times Christians confront people who aren't ready or willing to recognize their own problems. Those people cannot appreciate the value of our friendship or our rebuke. It's like offering expensive gems to farm animals—they don't know how to appreciate the true worth of what they've been given. Jesus was telling us that just because we *can* confront people, it's not always in our best interest to do so. Some people can't do anything with the advice or counsel we give, so why bother? We need to wait for the right time. Our goal is not to pick fights with people; our goal is to see peace restored between them and God (and also with other people who were offended by their actions).

Jesus also offers some thoughts on how to approach confrontation with fellow believers:

> If your brother sins against you, go and show him his fault, just between the two of you. If he listens to you, you have won your brother over. But if he will not lis-

What Does It Look Like to "Do Justice"?

ten, take one or two others along, so that "every matter may be established by the testimony of two or three witnesses." If he refuses to listen to them, tell it to the church; and if he refuses to listen even to the church, treat him as you would a pagan or a tax collector. (Matthew 18:15-17)

Jesus' words make sense in light of our goal of reconciliation. If someone wrongs you, you have a responsibility to go to that person and show him how he hurt you. Don't talk to your friends about it first. Don't let the problem fester. Just go and present your case to the person in private. Hopefully he'll see the error of his actions and seek your forgiveness in order to make things right. If that happens, reconciliation has been achieved.

If that doesn't happen, it's time to recruit two or three other people to hear the matter. Jesus doesn't mean you should gather others who feel the same as you do and "gang up" on the person. It's entirely possible that you've mistakenly or wrongly accused someone of hurting you, and maybe *you* need to see the matter more clearly. That's where wise and impartial mediators come in handy.

Should the impartial mediators agree that you've been wronged and if the person who offended you still refuses to listen to them, then it's obvious he doesn't value reconciliation and his heart isn't right. Therefore, you're free to take the matter to the entire church for consideration.

If the person rejects that as well, then Jesus says to kick him out of the congregation because he isn't a true brother in Christ. My experience has been that most people desire to restore fellowship with those they've wronged. They seldom allow situations to reach the point of church banishment. Remember, our goal is to restore relationships to God and other believers—not to punish, humiliate, or alienate.

So what about the people of the world—the "pagans" and "sinners" who haven't been reconciled to God yet? The Bible teaches us about that matter too:

> I have written you in my letter not to associate with sexually immoral people—not at all meaning the people of this world who are immoral, or the greedy and swindlers, or idolaters. In that case you would have to leave this world. But now I am writing you that you must not associate with anyone who calls himself a brother but is sexually immoral or greedy, an idolater or a slanderer, a drunkard or a swindler. With such a man do not even eat. What business is it of mine to judge those outside the church? Are you not to judge those inside? God will judge those outside. (1 Corinthians 5:9-13)

Paul wants us to know that while we must—for the sake of the work and the reputation of the church—hold other believers accountable, we aren't to judge the people of the world, people who are lost like we once were. Our goal is to help them know God and to see them reconciled to him.

Have I been clear so far? Doing justice is not about punishment, but about helping others restore their walk with God and with other people. God will do the punishing as he sees appropriate.

What Does It Look Like to "Do Justice"?

If only I'd known that when I read MB's note. Then my goal would not have been to embarrass or humiliate her, but to help restore her connection to God and to others. Imagine what a difference that might have made—in her life and in mine.

Questions to Ponder

1. How do you feel about what Mark did to his friend "MB"?

2. Have you ever acted in a judgmental manner?

3. Why is it so easy for people to judge others without even looking at their own lives?

4. List some situations in which it's okay, according to Scripture, to judge another person.

5. How is a Christian's wrongdoing different from that of a person who isn't a follower of Christ?

6. What should be the result of our justice?

YOU JUST GOTTA LOVE MERCY

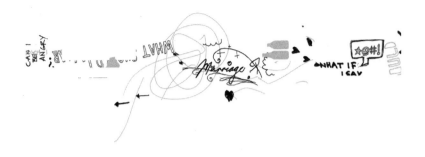

Growing up in a Christian home has its advantages. My parents were both *real* followers of Christ, as opposed to being "Sunday Christians" like a lot of people we knew. They were also good parents—something I've come to appreciate more and more as I grow older. I now realize that not everyone has that kind of home life.

What's more, becoming a follower of Christ at a young age meant that by the time I reached high school, I'd heard just about every story in the Bible. I'd also learned to make fairly good choices in my life. That's definitely a blessing. Strange as it may seem, though, I often felt as though I were a lesser Christian for having grown up in the church and in a strong Christian home.

I saw other kids my age—kids who didn't have parents in the church—come to know Christ, and I was amazed at how their lives changed. I became jealous of some of them. Their relationship with Jesus seemed more real than mine.

WHAT DOES GOD WANT FROM ME?

The way they lived displayed a level of authenticity that made my life seem fake by comparison. Seeing other people excited and joyful about their salvation actually made me feel a little anger toward God. After all, I'd been the "good boy" all along. Now these other people were stepping in after making some major screwups in their lives, and they actually seemed closer to God than I did. I wondered what was wrong with me that would cause God to ignore me.

At conferences and camps, I'd hear speakers give their testimonies about how they'd been axe-murdering, drug-doing, gas-station-robbing sinners who had sex with any-thing that moved—until they found Jesus, and then their lives changed. Tears filled their eyes as they talked about how they couldn't believe Jesus loved them enough to for-give their sins. Their passion often moved others to cry too. Tons of people would come forward after hearing these messages, wanting Jesus to change their lives as well.

I watched them from my seat, feeling as though I'd missed something. In fact, I thought God could never use me in ministry because I didn't have a cool story like the axe-murdering, drug-doing, gas-station-robbing sinners having sex with anything that moved who experienced sal-vation. If I got up to share my salvation story in front of a group, I'd have to say I asked my dad about Jesus when I was almost five. I'd say I knew Jesus wanted me to follow him, so I explained that to God during a prayer I said in my bathroom. And then the next day I went forward in church. Whoopee. That's not a very moving story.

You Just Gotta Love Mercy

Brainwashed?

One day when I was talking about Jesus with someone who wasn't a Christian, I got an odd response. The person I was trying to share my faith with accused me of being brainwashed by my family and church. He said if I'd grown up in a houseful of Hindus or Buddhists, then I'd be a Hindu or Buddhist.

The notion struck a chord with me. *Had I been brainwashed?* I wondered. Jesus' teachings always made sense to me and I really felt I believed them on my own. But the truth was, I didn't like who I was becoming. I was a bitter, angry, and not-very-loving person. But was I the problem? Or was the problem Jesus? I began to think that maybe I would've been better off finding Jesus when I was older, just so I'd know firsthand that all the drugs and sex and other things my friends had done before discovering the gospel was bad for me.

The fact was, I'd changed. I'd grown and matured. I wasn't a child any longer. And something dangerous had happened in my walk with God. I'd come to believe that I did good things because I was a genuinely good person, not because God called me to him at a young age. For as far back as I could remember, I'd been good in all the outwardly ways that people use to measure others.

Then I ran across this passage and it made me realize my problem:

At one time we too were foolish, disobedient, deceived and enslaved by all kinds of passions and pleasures. We lived in malice and envy, being hated and hating one another. But when the kindness and love of God our Savior appeared, he saved us, not because of righteous things we had done, but because of his mercy. (Titus 3:3-5)

I'd read those verses before, of course, but it never occurred to me that they might apply to me. I never thought I was guilty of any of those things. As far as I was concerned, I hadn't done much of anything wrong in my life. I never considered myself a slave to passions and pleasures. After all, I'd been a Christian since I was a kid.

After reading the passage in Titus anew, though, I had to admit that my walk with Christ had changed. I was becoming more evil in my heart and thoughts. I was envious of others—almost to the point of hating them. Christians were supposed to be moving away from such problems, but I seemed to be moving toward them.

The idea that my sin had been incredibly offensive to God and that I deserved death was new to me. Because Jesus saved me from my sin at such a young age, I couldn't fully comprehend the nature of my sin. I'd known what sin meant in the way a child knows what's wrong. But since my knowledge of God had increased, I'd never stopped to think about how amazing my salvation was. I knew some of my friends had been saved from some pretty dramatic sins (not to mention the whole axe-murdering, drug-doing, gas-station-robbing, having-sex-with-anything-that-moved crowd).

You Just Gotta Love Mercy

What I didn't realize is that I'd been saved from those things too—I was just saved *before* I experienced them.

I also realized with startling clarity that Jesus died for my awful sin, and it was only because of his mercy that I was able to be at peace with him and experience eternal life. Immediately, things began to click in my life. My new understanding of mercy created a new way of living. I became more merciful toward others. I came to really love mercy because now I was keenly aware that I'd also been a recipient of it. I wanted others to experience it too. But not just from me—because what good was my mercy? The mercy of Christ is what I wanted them to know.

Those Who Should Know Better

Apparently there were a lot of followers of God who grew up as I did. Jesus' harshest words were always directed toward those who should have known better—the teachers of the Law and the religious leaders of the day.

Jesus once told a story (in Matthew 18:23-35) about a man who owed a king an incredible sum of money—the equivalent of millions of dollars. Since people made little money in those days, the prospect of paying back a debt that large was impossible to imagine. One day the king decided to settle his accounts. He called for the man who owed the millions and asked him to pay up. Not surprisingly, the man didn't have the money to repay him. So the king ordered his family to be sold into slavery to pay the debt. Desperate, the man begged for mercy. Then the king took pity on the man and cleared his debt. He didn't simply reduce the amount of debt or give the man extra time to pay it off. Amazingly, the king *cancelled* the debt, wiped the record clean. And the man walked away debt free.

Jesus used the story to describe the debt he would later pay with his life. There's no way we could ever repay what we owe God for our sins. So God took the hit by sending Jesus to die for us. Amazing. But the story doesn't end there.

The man whose debt was cleared walked away from the king and went to see a friend who owed him some money. Compared to what the man owed the king, the amount of his friend's debt was insignificant—perhaps the equivalent of a buck seventy, the cost of a king-sized candy bar or a soda. But the friend couldn't repay even the small amount of money he owed, so the man had him thrown in prison.

Word soon traveled to the king about what had happened, and he was furious. He'd just forgiven that man millions in debt! The forgiven man should have thrown a party and been generous toward others. But he apparently didn't appreciate the mercy he'd received. So the king summoned the man and threw him into jail until he repaid all that he owed.

Ephesians 4:32 puts it this way: "Be kind and compassionate to one another, forgiving each other, just as in Christ God forgave you." *Grace* and *mercy* are two words that get confused a lot. Grace is when we get something we don't deserve. The gift of salvation is an act of grace because we receive the blood of Christ, payment for our sins, and the gift of eternal life—all of which we don't deserve. On the other hand, mercy is when we *don't* get what we deserve. As sinful people, we deserve to be punished and separated from God. But because God is merciful, Jesus was punished in our place so we don't get what we deserve. There are lots of people in the world—and in the church—who do things that deserve rude or hostile treatment from us. However, God calls us to be merciful, not to give others what they deserve.

I live in Texas, a state with some pretty slack gun laws. With a proper license, you can even carry a concealed weapon. One night at church we were talking about owning a gun. The people at my table were telling me they felt absolutely comfortable owning one for their protection. I explained that while I could use a gun to shoot tin cans off a fence, I couldn't see myself shooting another person.

One man was startled by my response. He asked, "If there were someone in your house harming your wife or children, you still wouldn't be able to shoot him?" My response was simple: "I don't think I could take a life." It was clear he didn't have a problem with the concept, especially if his family were in jeopardy. I told him the reason I couldn't do it is because I've received great mercy from God. I'd want the person invading my home also to experience the mercy I've experienced. Ending the person's life would seal his fate. Although I would go to extreme lengths to protect my family (or any victim of a crime), I couldn't intentionally take a human life—even if the person deserved it. I've been forgiven too much.

That's an extreme example and one I hope I'm never tested on. But every day we treat people based on what we think they deserve. That person wasn't smart with his money, so he deserves to be poor. Those people made bad choices, so they deserve the consequence of their decisions. She's rude to others, so she deserves to be shunned. The problem is, we're not supposed to give people what they deserve. As followers of God, we're called to do better than that. We're called to show mercy. God wants us to be merciful because he's been merciful to us. But if we don't appreciate his mercy, we won't show it to others.

Questions to Ponder

1. Mark grew up going to church regularly. How is his experience similar to or different from your own?

2. What advantages are there to growing up in the church? What advantages are there to finding Christ when you're older?

3. Have you ever wondered whether you were brainwashed into believing in Jesus? How are you certain you weren't?

4. What does God's mercy mean to you? When, if at all, did you realize what a great gift it is?

5. How should the gift of mercy change a person? Why do some people seem unchanged by it?

CHAPTER 8

WALKING HUMBLY WITH GOD

Sex, drugs, and rock 'n' roll were not issues I dealt with as I grew in my walk with God. No, my issues were not so easy to recognize or define. (After all, you either had sex, did drugs, and listened to bad music—or you didn't.) The sins I dealt with—pride and selfishness—were harder to nail down. They were sins of the heart and mind, not noticeable in my actions. I suppose that's why sins like greed, gossip, and arrogance run rampant in the church. They're hard to observe, and their consequences aren't immediately obvious. But they were my big problems, and the only people who cared enough to address them were my parents.

I'm definitely less prideful and arrogant than I was as a teenager. But like an alcoholic who longs for a drink every time he sees an ad for vodka, I continue to struggle with those issues even as an adult.

When I started out as a minister, I worked with another man. He'd speak and I'd do mini object lessons with magic tricks and other visual elements. While all of that was fun, I knew it wasn't my long-term calling in life. So I was excited when he let me speak during one of his slots at a university chapel. It was a great honor, and I put together (what I thought was) a powerful message from the Bible.

While my partner introduced me, I sat in the front pew of the chapel, getting ready to share. He gave me a huge build up and said many incredible things about me. And as I listened to him, I started feeling proud. I silently agreed with what he said. I even became convinced that when the people heard the words I was about to share, they'd know without a doubt that he'd spoken the truth about my greatness.

I was so into my partner's inflated words about me that I didn't realize my leg had fallen asleep. As everyone welcomed me with thunderous applause, I stood up from my seat—and fell flat on my face. My notes went flying everywhere. And you know that little dance you do to get the feeling back in your leg? That's what I did. I actually hopped around in circles in front of several hundred people.

I believe God did give me a good message to share that day; he just needed a more humble messenger to deliver it. And boy was I humbled when all those people laughed at me. Proverbs 16:18 says, "Pride goes before destruction, a haughty spirit before a fall." I know that all too well.

Walking Humbly with God

The Power of Humility

Micah says God wants us to do justice, love mercy, and walk humbly with God. Humility is a powerful character quality—one that, amazingly, Jesus himself possessed. Imagine being Jesus—the Son of God—and having to put up with inferior people who are prone to whining and asking stupid questions. If I'd been in Jesus' place when the Pharisees were questioning him, I'd have wanted to unleash my power with, say, laser beams shooting out of my hands, obliterating the questioners on the spot. Afterward, I'd have blown the smoke from my fingertips, looked up at the crowd, and asked, "Anyone else want to question whether or not I'm the Son of God?" That's probably how most of us would have dealt with the situation because we lack the humility Christ possessed.

The second chapter of Philippians reveals that Jesus didn't consider equality with God something to be grasped, even though he was equal to God in every way. Jesus had the same powers as God and deserved the same level of worship. Yet he never flaunted his deity. He didn't speak in a thundering voice. He wasn't accompanied by an angelic entourage blowing trumpets to announce his arrival. Instead, he lived as a human who was very devoted to God and his ways. He set a perfect example of humility for us.

Maybe you've heard the song lyric, "I cast all of my cares upon you." But did you know it comes from 1 Peter 5:6-7? Its words are linked to walking humbly with God, so let's check it out: "Humble yourselves, therefore, under

God's mighty hand, that he may lift you up in due time. Cast all your anxiety on him because he cares for you."

When I think of God's mighty hand, I picture huge hands like King Kong's. If you've seen the 2005 version of *King Kong*, think of the scene in which Ann Darrow (played by Naomi Watts) learns to trust Kong, despite being afraid of him. Though Kong's hands frightened her because of their power, she humbled herself so they could lift her up and carry her to the place he wanted to go.

Likewise, God wants to lead us through our lives. But in order for that to happen, we must humble ourselves before him so he'll put us in the place he has for us—in his time.

When I was in high school I didn't date much. I was okay with that, for the most part. But it did make me wonder what was wrong with me. Why didn't I have all the babes like some of my friends? I wasn't attracted to the girls who were interested in me, and the girls I liked weren't into me. My buddies would go out with their girlfriends on the weekends, and I'd stay home by myself. I'll admit it—I cried sometimes. It was that painful. But at the same time, I knew God was doing other things in my life. I trusted him. When the time was right, God did bring girls into my life. Looking back, I'm glad they didn't come around any sooner. Girls require an investment of money and time. So before I began dating, God had me doing other things with my free time that became important in how he wanted to use me later on.

Walking Humbly with God

Humbling yourself before God and trusting him to do what he wants with your life whenever he wants to do it may create some anxiety. I've talked to guys who said if they trusted God to help them find their spouses, they'd be afraid he'd only pick girls with a "nice personality." Our natural instinct is to want to run our own lives, but this call to walk humbly with God means we have to trust him.

The anxiety caused by our humility is what that song talks about. You can cast all your anxiety on the Lord. Why? Because he cares for you. God doesn't want you to marry someone you aren't attracted to. He doesn't want your life to be unfulfilling. He doesn't want you to be bored. He wants the best for you.

The Daily Journey

Walking humbly is not a one-time event; it's a daily journey. To lose sight of humility is to set yourself up for a major fall. Many of God's followers have made terrible mistakes later in their lives—when you'd think they'd know better. And most of those mistakes can be attributed to a lack of humility.

Often we deceive ourselves into believing we're walking humbly, when in fact we aren't. The opposite of walking humbly is living life in our own strength—in other words, living like we want to because we're fairly confident we can. Consider the following examples of Chris and Chelsea. Which one is walking humbly with God?

Chris is a good athlete who plays just about every sport well. When it comes to baseball, however, Chris is beyond good—he's amazing. Generally speaking, as the seasons change, so do the sports Chris is involved with. This year, however, he's been asked to play baseball in a special club league. It's a step up from the normal high school league, so Chris decides to do it. Is he walking humbly with God?

Chelsea is graduating from high school this year and she's trying to figure out what she should do with her summer before college begins. She'd like to get a job to earn some extra money, but she also has an opportunity to serve at a summer camp that her church runs for children with special needs. Realizing it may be her last summer to do camp, she decides to serve there. Is Chelsea walking humbly?

From the little bit we know about these two situations, it's difficult to make a definitive determination, but it would appear that neither Chris nor Chelsea is walking humbly with God. Both approached their decisions from the perspective of what *they* felt was right or what made sense to *them*. Neither seemed to depend much on God for guidance. At the same time, with a little more information about how they came to make the choices they did, we might determine that both were walking humbly with God. (Note: the fact that Chelsea's decision led her to choose church camp over a summer job doesn't automatically mean she was walking humbly with God.)

Some passages in Scripture show us the way to walk humbly with God. Proverbs 3:5-6 says, "Trust in the Lord with all your heart and lean not on your own understanding;

Walking Humbly with God

in all your ways acknowledge him, and he will make your paths straight." Do you see that word *lean*? Think about the things you lean on. I've leaned on (among other things) a tree, the side of a building, a doorframe, and a countertop. In a sense, every time I've sat in a chair, I've "leaned" my body weight on it for its support.

As a kid I can remember rocking on the back legs of my chair at the dining room table. My dad scolded me and told me I needed to sit "with all four on the floor." But regardless of his constant rebukes, I continued leaning back on the two legs. They seemed strong enough to me, and I enjoyed reclining at that angle. You know what happened next, don't you? One night the chair collapsed at the dinner table and I fell to the floor. The chair itself was not faulty; my understanding of it was. I was using it in a manner for which it was not designed.

Far too often we think, act, and make life choices based on how WE perceive life works. That is a certain way to become proud. While God has created us as unique people and has given us different paths to walk, he and his wisdom are consistent. They don't change. Because of this, we can trust in God. We can lean on his wisdom, his understanding of life. We can be secure, not falling over.

Our Proper Place

When we're walking humbly, we're constantly mindful of our proper place in God's universe. When I was in college at Biola University in Southern California, I'd often go to the beach with my friends. One particular night I was lying near the breaking tide. The sky was filled with stars; it was an exceptionally clear night. The moon wasn't quite half full, but it had a three-dimensional shading to it. It looked like a sphere, rather than an illuminated flat circle. With no trees, cliffs, or buildings nearby, I felt as though there were nothing between the moon and me but space. I imagined myself sticking to the surface of the globe. I was literally on the edge of California, the ocean just a few feet away. If I'd rolled over a couple times, I'd have fallen right off the continent and into the Pacific Ocean. I realized how small I was and how infinite the universe was. It was mind-blowing—and very humbling. (And I accomplished all of it without hallucinogenic drugs.)

As I laid there, I recalled Psalm 8:3-4: "When I consider your heavens, the work of your fingers, the moon and the stars, which you have set in place, what is man that you are mindful of him, the son of man that you care for him?" God knows the number of stars that were in the sky that night. He knows the number of hairs on my head and the number of grains of sand under my feet. How amazing is it to understand that the God of the universe knows us and cares for us?

In Psalm 8:5-6 David continues, "You made him [humans] a little lower than the heavenly beings and crowned him with glory and honor. You made him ruler over the works of your hands; you put everything under his feet." Having the knowledge that all creation belongs to God—the One who made it—should help keep us humble. So should the real-

Walking Humbly with God

ization that any authority or power we have over creation was given to us by God.

David's son Solomon, who wrote the book of Proverbs, understood this. In 1 Kings 3, Solomon takes over the kingship of Israel from his father. But Solomon realizes that God made him king and Solomon isn't capable of leading the nation on his own. So when God tells Solomon to ask for anything he wants, Solomon asks for a discerning heart to govern God's people and be able to distinguish between right and wrong. Solomon asked for wisdom, to be able to see and understand life the way God sees it. His request was an incredible act of humility.

However, walking humbly requires more than humility. While Solomon began his reign well, he eventually began to lean on his own understanding again. And he got himself into some serious trouble along the way. It's not enough to *know* that God rules over all, we must also demonstrate it in the way we live.

Let's walk humbly together in the knowledge and presence of God.

Questions to Ponder

1. On a scale of one to ten, how prideful are you? Ask a friend who knows you well to answer that question about you. Then ask someone who doesn't know you well to answer that same question.

2. Is it easy for you to trust God as you walk through life? Why or why not? What's the hardest thing to trust God for?

3. Can you remember a time when you realized you were acting in your own strength rather than walking humbly with God? If so, what happened?

4. What's the difference between being humble before God and not taking responsibility for your own actions?

Walking Humbly with God

CHAPTER

9

PEOPLE VERSUS PEOPLES:
GOD'S COMMISSION TO THOSE
WHO FOLLOW HIM

When I was a kid, my dad would often read to my brothers and me at bedtime. Sitting in a rocking chair by the door, he'd read Bible stories and books such as the Chronicles of Narnia series by C.S. Lewis. My favorite stories, though, were the biographies of missionaries who lived amazing lives in God's service. I remember hearing about the adventures of Adoniram Judson, Jim Elliot, Hudson Taylor, and others who served God in foreign lands. Their stories taught me that following Christ isn't an easy thing to do. Many of the missionaries I learned about endured pain and suffering in their efforts to be obedient to God and walk humbly with him.

The stories of these great missionaries also caused me to realize how big this God thing really is. It wasn't just my church or my town that was involved; Jesus Christ wanted *everyone* to know about him. And because of my dad's efforts to read to my family, I knew God wasn't just interested in *people*, but *peoples*—with an *s*.

WHAT DOES GOD WANT FROM ME?

Scattered

How much do you know about the Tower of Babel, the place where God confused human speech and established a multi-lingual world? In order to fully understand what happened at Babel, you have to go back to God's first command to his human creation. In Genesis 1:28 God made it clear that he wanted humans to fill the earth. All of it. Humans, however, had a different plan.

Genesis 11 tells us most people shared the same language and had no desire to scatter or fill the earth. Instead, they started to work on a tower that would reach the heavens. The tower's construction was more than just a building project; it was an act of defiance toward God. That's why he confused their languages and caused people to separate and spread out. His desire was for people to become diverse, not homogeneous (that is, all the same).

While God's plan called for diversity, God never intended for these newly formed people groups to become islands either, cut off from all interaction with each other. When the time came to reveal himself, God's plan called for the whole world to come to know him—through the work of his chosen people. In Genesis 12:1-3 God made a covenant with Abraham in which he promised to make a nation out of Abraham's descendants and bless the people of that nation—the nation of Israel. God wasn't playing favorites; his plan was to reveal himself to all nations through Israel.

Consider how Egypt learned of the Lord God during the times of Joseph and Moses. Babylon learned of him through

Daniel, Shadrach, Meshach, and Abednego. Assyria learned of him through the prophet Jonah. The Queen of Sheba learned of him through King Solomon. What's more, God promised that salvation (in the form of his Son Jesus Christ) would come via the people of Israel.

In the New Testament, we see the ultimate evidence of God's love for humankind through the birth, life, and death of Jesus. When Jesus went to the cross to die, he didn't do it just for the sins of Israel, but for the sins of all humanity. Then before he returned to heaven, Jesus gave his disciples a command, a commission—something to do before he returns to earth a second time. We call this the Great Commission and it can be found in Matthew 28:18-20:

> Then Jesus came to them and said, "All authority in heaven and on earth has been given to me. Therefore go and make disciples of all nations, baptizing them in the name of the Father and of the Son and of the Holy Spirit, and teaching them to obey everything I have commanded you. And surely I am with you always, to the very end of the age."

In these verses we see another example of what God wants from us. He wants us to share with all the peoples of the world what Jesus has done. He wants us to help others follow him. Notice how Jesus doesn't tell us to go and make disciples of people. He specifically requires us to go to all nations, the "peoples" of the world. It's great to share God's love with people who are close to us, but the Lord also wants us to be about reaching those who aren't like us.

One God, Many Ways to Worship

When I was in high school, I took a trip to Haiti to see what God was doing there and to lend a hand to a growing Haitian church. Though the Haitians generally did the same things we do—eat, sleep, work, play, worship, and spend time with their family and friends—I was struck by the differences between our two cultures. The food they ate was much different from the food I typically ate. (I liked their food better than much of what I ate at home—sorry, Mom.) The games they played were different from the games my friends and I played. We even had different ways of expressing the same needs and desires. And my Haitian friends had some really keen insights into God and Scripture that I'd never considered before. It soon became apparent to me that I needed those people in my life—and I hoped they needed me too.

When I returned home, my eyes had been opened. I noticed that even among the different ethnicities in my area, church was different. Some of my Hispanic friends spent all day Sunday with the members of their church family. Their all-day-party church atmosphere was a sharp contrast to the quick-bolt-to-lunch tendencies I'd observed after a Sunday morning service at my church. Likewise, the worship in a nearby African-American church was totally different from the worship in my mostly white church. My African-American friends really rocked the house when they sang. The energy their pastor displayed as he shared his sermon inspired me in ways my pastor never did. And my Korean friends were very concerned about holiness and would go on prayer-and-fasting retreats—something I couldn't imagine anyone in my youth group doing.

I'm sure problems existed in those other churches, just as they did in mine. (All churches are made up of imperfect people, after all.) And I'm sure my church offered many things that other churches lacked. The point is, we all had something to learn from each other and something to share that intensified and enriched our worship of God.

In college I heard an illustration that really helped me understand why "peoples" are important to God. Imagine that our reality (little "r" reality) exists under a colander (that bowl-like kitchen utensil with holes in the bottom; you use it to rinse and drain pasta and other foods), and God's Reality (big "R" reality) encompasses everything outside of the colander. Every person underneath that colander is looking up through a different hole and seeing a unique perspective of God. As we come together to share our perspectives—and learn to see through different holes—we get a more complete view of God and his Word. Pretty cool, huh?

The problem is, many Christians today are about as interested in diversity as the builders of the Tower of Babel were. The truth is, most of us prefer to be around people who are more like us. That's where the commonality of Christ that we share with other believers should come into play. But many self-professed Christians fail to make their Christianity the central part of their lives. Their faith is made up of very little that influences the way they live 24/7. And that's a big problem. If Christ isn't your center, then you won't experience a common bond when you meet believers who are different from you.

I've seen it happen countless times on mission trips. People who are very weak in their understanding of Christ develop little or no connection with the people they came to serve. After spending thousands of dollars and weeks of their own time, after enduring personal hardship to serve others in a country very different from their own, they walk away virtually unchanged. It only takes the flight home to make them forget everything about the brothers and sisters in Christ they served.

I've experienced that kind of short-term memory loss myself. Remember the mission trip I told you about in chapter 1—the one I signed up for only because I thought a hot girl in my youth group had signed up to go too? That entire trip barely registered with me. I got out of it exactly what I put into it—nothing. What a wasted opportunity!

Changes

Earlier I told you about some of the missionaries my father introduced me to through books. Because of their obedience and the obedience of thousands of others over the last 100 years, the world has been changed. It used to be that if you were going to hear about the gospel of Jesus Christ, it would come from a white-skinned person who hailed from the United States or somewhere in Europe. But all that has changed. India and the African nations now send more missionaries into the world than the United States does. It also used to be that 70 percent of all Christians lived in the Western world. Now the opposite is the case. Most Christians in our world today live below the equator.

While it's really cool to see the Great Commission moving forward, we American Christians need to rethink our attitude toward Jesus' command. For some reason we began to believe we were God's hope for the world—and that's clearly not the case. Today the most effective mission work involves disciples of Christ from many nations working together to reach others. One organization in particular that fits the bill is The Seed Company, part of Wycliffe Bible Translators.

For decades the "Wycliffe way" of Bible translation was to send a missionary to a foreign land where he would learn the language, translate the Bible, and help get it into people's hands. But as Christianity spread, Wycliffe saw the need to adapt its strategies. The organization now looks for Christians living in areas that have no native-tongue Bibles. Those native believers are then trained to assist in the translation process. They play a key role in making the Bible accessible to their people.

The Seed Company is one of Wycliffe's offshoot organizations, and it's dedicated to helping connect God's people to do the work of Bible translation (For more information, check out www.oneverse.org.). It's amazing to see God work through the efforts of his people. And The Seed Company is just one example.

For all that's been done so far, though, there's still a lot of work left to do. Population figures tell us there are approximately 6,912 languages in the world today. Approximately 1,678 of them will die out in the next decade, leaving about 5,234. Of those, about 422 already have a complete version of the Bible. Approximately 1,079 of them have a New Testament, and 1,204 have translation projects in the works.

That leaves 2,529 people groups in this world with no form of Scripture and no translation in progress. That's one of the needs we're up against.

If 2,529 languages seems like a lot to you, consider this: Wycliffe Bible Translators believe it's possible to have New Testaments completed (or at least started) in every one of those languages by 2025—if the church around the world works together. That's a pretty amazing statement—and one that should inspire each of us to get involved in some way. How can you pray? What can you give? Where can you go serve—either for a short time or for a lifetime? What does God want from you?

Jesus said, "The harvest is plentiful but the workers are few. Ask the Lord of the harvest to send out workers into his harvest field" (Matthew 9:37-38). Many people are ready to learn about the one true living God and his Son who died for their sins. Will you pray that God will send workers into the field? Are you ready to become one of those workers?

People Versus Peoples: God's Commission to Those Who Follow Him

Questions to Ponder

1. How is "making disciples" similar to or different from sharing one's faith?

2. How seriously do you take Jesus' command to make disciples? Explain.

3. How actively does your church pursue or support cross-cultural missions?

4. What are three ways your life will be different because you've read this book?

5. What are three things you'll do as a result of what you've learned?

MOVIES AND TV PROGRAMS THAT GLORIFY WITCHCRAFT AND
OCCULT PRACTICES ARE SUCKING TEENAGERS JUST LIKE YOU
INTO A WEB OF LIES. THIS BOOK DRAWS A CLEAR DISTINCTION
BETWEEN WHAT'S REAL AND WHAT'S NOT; WHAT THE BIBLE SAYS,
AND WHAT IT DOESN'T SAY WHEN IT COMES TO THE
SUPERNATURAL.

Don't Buy the Lie
Discerning Truth in a World of Deception
Mark Matlock

RETAIL $9.99
ISBN 0-310-25814-6

ECCLESIASTES IS ABOUT A KING WHO TRIED EVERYTHING AND
CAME TO A RADICAL CONCLUSION ABOUT HOW LIFE SHOULD BE
LIVED.

LIVING A LIFE THAT MATTERS HELPS YOU MAKE SENSE OF
SOLOMON'S EXPERIENCES, LEADS YOU TO MEANING IN YOUR
OWN LIFE, AND GIVES YOU THE TOOLS TO HELP YOUR FRIENDS
DO THE SAME.

Living a Life That Matters
Lessons from Solomon—the Man Who Tried Everything

Mark Matlock

RETAIL $9.99
ISBN 0-310-25816-2

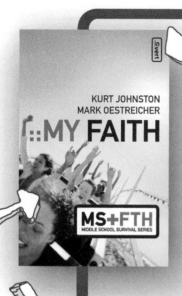

KURT JOHNSTON
MARK OESTREICHER

::MY FAITH

MS+FTH
MIDDLE SCHOOL SURVIVAL SERIES

LIFE AND FAITH CAN BE HARD WHEN
YOU'RE IN MIDDLE SCHOOL. BUT THIS
BOOK GIVES YOU ALL THE TIPS AND
SECRETS YOU NEED TO REALLY GRASP
YOUR FAITH AND KEEP HOLD OF IT.

My Faith
Middle School Survival Series
Kurt Johnston & Mark Oestreicher

RETAIL $9.99
ISBN 0-310-27382-X

KURT JOHNSTON
MARK OESTREICHER

::MY FAMILY

MS+FTH
MIDDLE SCHOOL SURVIVAL SERIES

EVERYTHING IS CHANGING—INCLUDING
THE WAY YOUR FAMILY INTERACTS.
THIS BOOK WILL GIVE YOU SECRETS
AND TIPS TO HELP MAKE YOUR FAMILY
EVEN BETTER AND SURVIVE THE
CHANGES THAT COME ALONG WITH
MIDDLE SCHOOL.

My Family
Middle School Survival Series
Kurt Johnston & Mark Oestreicher

RETAIL $9.99
ISBN 0-310-27430-3

invert

Visit www.invertbooks.com or your local bookstore.

LISTEN TO WHAT JESUS HAS TO SAY TO YOU. IN THIS 60-DAY
DEVO YOU'LL RECEIVE DAILY LETTERS FROM JESUS AND
SPEND SOME TIME JOURNALING YOUR THOUGHTS BACK TO
HIM AS YOU TAKE PART IN THE CONVERSATION.

Conversations with Jesus
Getting in on God's Story
Youth for Christ

RETAIL $10.99
ISBN 0-310-27346-3

invert

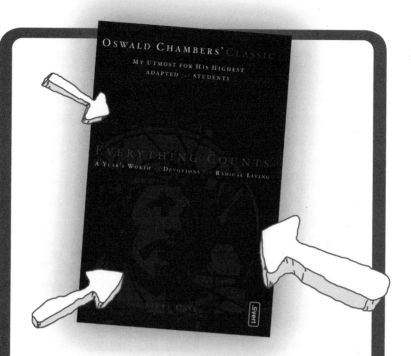

THE CLASSIC OSWALD CHAMBERS' *MY UTMOST FOR HIS HIGHEST* ADAPTED FOR STUDENTS, THIS DAILY DEVOTIONAL DUMPS THE PLEASANTRIES OF RELIGION AND LEADS YOUR STUDENTS TO REAL FAITH. EACH DAY INCLUDES A SCRIPTURE REFERENCE, AN EXCERPT FROM THE CLASSIC TEXT, AND A PHRASE STUDENTS CAN EASILY MEMORIZE TO REMIND THEM ABOUT THE REALITY OF BEING A CHILD OF GOD.

Everything Counts
A Year's Worth of Devotions on Radical Living
Steven Case

RETAIL $14.99
ISBN 0-310-25408-6

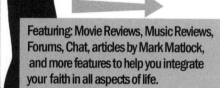

INTRODUCING THE ONLY NIV BIBLE SPECIFICALLY FOR TEEN
GUYS AGES 13-16. REVOLUTION REVEALS GOD AS THE ULTIMATE
REVOLUTIONARY AND PROVIDES A ROAD MAP FOR EVERY GUY TO
LIVE A REVOLUTIONARY, HARD-HITTING, DIFFERENCE-MAKING
LIFE BY READING HIS BIBLE. THIS BIBLE INCLUDES SPECIAL
FEATURES THAT ADDRESS RELEVANT ISSUES FACING GUYS
TODAY: FRIENDS THAT GET THEM INTO TROUBLE, ENEMIES WHO
MAKE LIFE MISERABLE FOR THEM, RULES THAT SEEM TO SPOIL
THEIR FUN, PARENTS WHO DON'T UNDERSTAND, AND MORE.

REVOLUTION HAS LOADS OF SPECIAL FEATURES AND AN
INFORMATIVE WEB SITE WITH ADDITIONAL RESOURCES ON MANY
OF THE FEATURE TOPICS, BIBLE READING PLANS, LINKS TO
OTHER SITES AND MORE!

Revolution SC
The NIV Bible for Teen Guys
Livingstone Corporation, General Editor

RETAIL $22.99
ISBN 0-310-92820-6

Visit www.invertbooks.com or your local bookstore.